Healthy Soul Food Cooking

Fabiola D. Gaines, RD, LD
Roniece A. Weaver, MS, RD, LD

SMALL STEPS PRESS

Director, Book Publishing, John Fedor; *Managing Editor, Book Publishing,* Abe Ogden; *Acquisitions Editor, Consumer Books,* Robert Anthony; *Editor,* Greg Guthrie; *Production Manager,* Melissa Sprott; *Composition,* American Diabetes Association; *Cover Design,* Koncept, Inc.; *Printer,* Transcontinental Printing.

Printed in Canada
1 3 5 7 9 10 8 6 4 2

Small Steps Press is an imprint of the American Diabetes Association. For information about Small Steps Press or the American Diabetes Association, in English or Spanish, call 1-800-342-2383. To order other Small Steps books, call 1-800-232-6733.

Consult a health care professional before trying any of the suggestions in this publication. Small Steps Press and the American Diabetes Association assume no responsibility for any injury that may result from the suggestions or information in this publication.

♾ The paper in this publication meets the requirements of the ANSI Standard Z39.48-1992 (permanence of paper).

Small Steps Press titles may be purchased for business or promotional use or for special sales. To purchase more than 50 copies of this book at a discount, or for custom editions of this book with your logo, contact Lee Romano Sequeira, Special Sales & Promotions, at the address below, or at LRomano@diabetes.org or 703-299-2046.

For all other inquiries, please call 1-800-DIABETES.

Small Steps Press
1701 North Beauregard Street
Alexandria, Virginia 22311

Library of Congress Cataloging-in-Publication Data

Gaines, Fabiola, 1952-
  Healthy soul food cooking / Fabiola D. Gaines and Roniece Weaver.
      p. cm.
  Includes bibliographical references and index.
  ISBN 978-1-58040-227-9 (alk. paper)
  1. Diabetes--Diet therapy--Recipes. 2. African American cookery. I. Weaver, Roniece, 1960- II. Title.

  RC662.G345 2007
  641.5'6314--dc22
                                        2006034814

To my parents, Bernetha Sirmans Demps and John L. Demps, Sr. Your spirits will be forever with me.

—Fabiola

To Dad and Mom. Daddy, I know you're not here to see my joy, but your spirit is alive and well in me. Thank you for your inspirational thoughts and words of encouragement. Mom, you are truly the best. Thank you for listening to me and being a stabilizing force. God has blessed me in that I have come into this world through the both of you.

—Roniece

Contents

Preface

It's hard for us to think of anyone we know who hasn't been touched by health issues and disease in some way. We have spent years learning how to help people develop healthier ways of eating so they can avoid the long-term consequences of poor health. Our knowledge doesn't just come from learning and training; it also comes from personal experience. We have lived through much of what you may be going through now, and we know it's not easy to make some of the lifestyle changes you need to make.

Roniece remembers when her dad suddenly began to eat more sweets and complain of tiredness and blurry vision. Everyone tried to ignore these strange signs, until the day her dad didn't get up to go to work. He found out he had diabetes and was told to go on insulin, a special diet, and exercise. The first Sunday morning after his diagnosis, as he reached for the familiar biscuits, butter, bacon, and syrup that he had every Sunday, Roniece began to cry. Her father looked at her in amazement. "I'm the one who should be crying, not you!" he said. "Everybody has taken everything I love away from me!" But he left the table without eating more.

Fabiola's father was diagnosed with diabetes after a heart attack, but he was determined to avoid insulin shots. She watched as he struggled to come to terms with the inadequate instruction he received on diet and exercise. The rest of the family had to do without their favorite sweets and desserts, until the day her mother made her special sweet potato pie and served her dad a piece. He objected and said, "Are you trying to kill me? That pie is not on my meal plan!" After a year, her dad was controlling his diabetes through diet and exercise alone, and Fabiola was learning how far a little determination and education can help someone go.

There are millions of people in our African-American community with undiagnosed and untreated health issues, especially diabetes. Worse, there are those who don't know how to make the small changes that are necessary for a healthy lifestyle. We wrote this book to help you learn how to eat better without giving up the traditional flavors you have grown up with and that you love. We want you to know that you can live long, healthy lives and that soul food doesn't have to be cut out of your diet. You can do this. You have the strength to meet this challenge, and we hope you will enjoy these recipes for many, many years.

Acknowledgments

This cookbook would not have been possible without the love and support of many people. Thank you for assisting me in this endeavor. Your time, patience, and recipes have been invaluable. I thank my soul mate, Charlie A. Gaines, III, whom I love for many reasons. If not for your guidance, support, teaching, and reasoning, I would have given up. You kept me going through those late-night sessions. Thank you for being the wonderful man you are. I want to thank my adult children (I know you wanted me to put that in), Devona and Tramaine, for the many times you just left me alone. You are wonderful children, and I am so proud of both of you. My mother-in-law, Mary Alice Gaines, kept me on my toes while trying to keep her blood sugars under control. Thank you for your prayers and guidance. Thanks to Audrey Allison for the long, tireless nights of typing while we worked on revisions. I thank my siblings, John L. Demps, Jr., Jeanette Demps Hudson, and Eunice Demps, for the memories of stress-free days and laughter. Thanks to Cynthia Holmes for believing in me. I appreciate the support and love of my aunts and uncles on the Demps, Holmes, and Sirmans sides of the family. Deborah Jean Mitchell, Vavescia Johnson, Felecia Williams, and Almeda Jefferson: thank you for being the best friends a girl could have. Thanks to the American Diabetes Association of Orlando for believing in us and giving us the opportunity to make a difference in our community. Finally, thanks to the American Diabetes Association, National Office, for the freedom to create this book and for giving us the chance to get the message out.

—Fabiola

My heartfelt thanks go to my husband, Dr. Curtis Weaver, for reading this book and lending a strong shoulder so I could finish it. Thanks also go to the loves of my life, my children, Candace and Curtis (CJ), for giving me the time I needed to be alone. Thanks go to my sisters, Willa Ashe, Althea Howell, and Rojean Williams, for your input and words of encouragement. You all have been an irreplaceable cheerleading section. Thanks go to my loving in-laws and friends, Zelma Weaver, Isabella Christian, Michael Weaver, Julia Weaver, Everette Howell, and Daughn Cantrell, for sharing your family recipes. Glenn Barbour, thanks for the many times you inspired me to continue with this project. Your energy is contagious. I thank the Reverend Walter R. Prince, pastor of Mt. Pleasant Missionary Baptist Church of Orlando, Florida, for your spiritual guidance and uplifting words that inspire me to continue to grow and be creative. You have taught me to have faith and believe that through God, all things are possible. Thank you for the hours you put into this book. I appreciate the support of the Mt. Pleasant Missionary Baptist Church family and the opportunity to work with the congregation, Silver Angels, and many other projects. I am proud to say that my church home is one that practices "heart healthy" deeds of service. Thanks go to Deaconesses Della Fayson and Mary Key, Deacon Perry Bell, and Bishop Simon Peter Mabson for sharing your stories with me. Sherman Sheffield made us look great in print—you're the best. Lorraine Onfroy, CDE; the American Diabetes Association in Orlando; Delia Javier; and Nancy Carlton offered their kind support from the very beginning. We continue to appreciate their input and assistance. The Orlando Regional Medical Center Diabetes Treatment Center of Orlando offered clinical opinions and thoughtful revisions. Thanks for the collaborative input. God put Parniece Spears and Edward J. Thompson in my path at a special time in my life. Thank you for your friendship. My deepest appreciation goes to my many special friends who were there for late-night talks or e-mail conversations. You are all jewels that will always shine in the window to my heart. I love you all.

—Roniece

A Note about Food Labels

Many food labels in the grocery store use terms that can be confusing. However, you're going to find that food labels are your best friends when it comes to following a healthy diet. To help you shop healthier, here is a list of the common terms as defined by the U.S. Food and Drug Administration.

Sugar

Sugar Free: Less than 0.5 grams of sugar per serving.

No Added Sugar, Without Added Sugar, No Sugar Added: This does not mean the same as "sugar free." A label bearing these words means that no sugars were added during processing or that processing does not increase the sugar content above the amount that the ingredients naturally contain. Consult the nutrition information panel to see the total amount of sugar in the product.

Reduced Sugar: At least 25% less sugar per serving than the regular product.

Calories

Calorie Free: Fewer than 5 calories per serving.

Low Calorie: 40 calories or less per serving. (If servings are smaller than 30 grams, or smaller than 2 tablespoons, this means 40 calories or less per 50 grams of food.)

Reduced Calorie, Fewer Calories: At least 25% fewer calories per serving than the regular product.

Fat

Fat Free, Nonfat: Less than 0.5 gram of fat per serving.

Low Fat: 3 grams or less of fat per serving. (If servings are smaller than 30 grams, or smaller than 2 tablespoons, this means 3 grams or less of fat per 50 grams of food.)

Reduced Fat, Less Fat: At least 25% less fat per serving than the regular product.

Cholesterol

Cholesterol Free: Less than 2 milligrams of cholesterol and 2 grams or less of saturated fat per serving.

Low Cholesterol: 20 milligrams or less of cholesterol and 2 grams or less of saturated fat per serving.

Reduced Cholesterol, Less Cholesterol: At least 25% less cholesterol and 2 grams or less of saturated fat per serving than the regular product.

Sodium

Sodium Free: Less than 5 milligrams of sodium per serving.

Low Sodium: 140 milligrams or less of sodium per serving.

Very Low Sodium: 35 milligrams or less of sodium per serving.

Reduced Sodium, Less Sodium: At least 25% less sodium per serving than the regular product.

Light or Lite Foods

Foods that are labeled "Light" or "Lite" are usually either lower in fat or lower in calories than the regular product. Some products may also be lower in sodium. Check the nutrition information label on the product to be sure how much is really contained in the food you're buying.

Meat and Poultry

Lean: Less than 10 grams of fat, 4.5 grams or less of saturated fat, and less than 95 milligrams of cholesterol per serving and per 100 grams.

Extra Lean: Less than 5 grams of fat, less than 2 grams of saturated fat, and less than 95 milligrams of cholesterol per serving and per 100 grams.

Introduction

The tradition of African-American cookery is a long one, steeped in ancient history, recent tribulation, and abiding faith. From its roots in grain-producing civilizations in Egypt, through its transformation by contact with European cultures, and during its wrenching evolution caused by the largest forced uprooting of a group of people that has ever occurred in history, African-American culture has survived, nowhere more obviously than in its cuisine.

African slaves became the gardeners and cooks of the Southern plantations and, once freed, migrated north and west to work as chuck wagon cooks, railroad chefs, nightclub hosts, and restaurant owners. New geographical influences were integrated with old cooking traditions, methods, and techniques to create constantly evolving flavor combinations. Other recipes were passed from generation to generation and remained virtually unchanged for hundreds of years. Modern soul food cooking represents the best of the melding of old and new, of past and present cooking practices.

When the first slaves arrived in Virginia in 1619, it was a matter of survival to take whatever scraps were available and make them palatable. Common foods included rice, beans, cornmeal, black-eyed peas, sweet potatoes (which replaced the African yam), greens and onions grown in backyard gardens, okra, chilies from the Caribbean (a cheap way to add flavor to food), meat scraps (usually "fatback" from hogs), and molasses.

Diets were predominantly vegetarian, with some fish, possum, or squirrel for flavor. Foods were boiled, fried, roasted, or baked. Stews and thick gumbos, the liberal use of molasses, and fat-laden gravies provided calories. African Americans used salt and sweeteners in abundance without suffering from any ill health because of the countless hours spent in hard manual labor.

The strong tradition of the family established in Africa abides today in shared meals at home, church, and restaurants, where the cooking is often collective and the food sustains the spirit as well as the body. But modern African Americans have new health concerns not shared by their ancestors. The liberal use of salt and sweeteners in traditionally prepared foods is killing us. We can avoid much of the hypertension, heart disease, diabetes, and other diseases plaguing us by making simple modifications to our meal plans and cooking styles. If you're at risk for any of these conditions, we can show you how to make some simple changes to your soul food without losing too much of the flavor and tradition you love.

Accepting the Truth

The first thing you need to do is accept the fact that you should be following a healthy diet. Realizing this does not mean the end of life as you know it—only that, with some lifestyle changes, you can avoid some of the scary diseases that may have afflicted some of your loved ones. Accepting the truth means working through these feelings in order to take care of yourself and live a full life.

If you find yourself saying "one bite won't hurt," "I'll go to the doctor later," "my condition isn't serious," or "my medication will take care of this," you could be in denial about your health. Try talking to other people about how they cope with their situation. Tell your friends and family what you need to do to take care of yourself. Accept that it may take some time to adapt to this news.

If you're angry or depressed, try some ways to defuse your feelings. Move around, breathe deeply, go see a movie, go for a walk with a loved one. Talk about it with someone or try to see the larger picture. Let your depression fade and use your anger to become stronger and more determined to become healthier.

Now What?

You met with your doctor to learn all you can about your condition. Your doctor might refer you to a dietitian, who can help you plan meals and snacks to optimize your health. You'll likely want to begin an easy exercise program and, if you do, stop smoking. Your goals may include:

- Learning all you can about your condition from many sources
- Getting a tasty meal plan from a registered dietitian
- Maintaining a healthy weight by eating a variety of small, frequent meals
- Starting a healthy exercise routine
- Stopping unhealthy habits, such as smoking
- Taking the proper medications
- Getting annual examinations from a specialist
- Establishing long- and short-term goals for your self-care

Sometimes the hardest goal of all can be changing how you eat. You may believe you need to eliminate every food you love to be healthy. That's just not true. You can learn to integrate many of your old favorites into a healthy meal plan and add new versions of foods that taste just as good as the way you used to prepare them.

What Can I Eat?

You can eat many of your old favorites, with just a few simple ingredient substitutions that won't change the flavor as much as you might think. For example, use smoked turkey instead of bacon with vegetables, canola oil instead of lard for fritters, and fruit spreads instead of syrup on biscuits. Making these substitutions may feel like a chore, but if you do, you'll find that you feel better, look better, and have more energy when following a healthy meal plan.

Help with Meal Planning

There are several tools to help you follow a successful meal plan. We'll describe some of the more popular methods for you here: Exchange Lists, carbohydrate counting, and using the Soul Food Pyramid.

Exchange Lists

Exchange Lists are lists of foods that have been sorted by type and amount of nutrient. One serving of a food on a list has about the same amount of calories, protein, fat, and carbohydrate as the other foods on the list and can be "exchanged" or traded based on what you feel like eating that day.

For example, whole-wheat bread, waffles, sugar-frosted cereal, baked potatoes, and corn are all on the starch list. Your meal plan calls for a piece of toast for breakfast, but you feel like eating a waffle. You can trade one for the other, as long as you pay attention to the serving size (one piece of whole-wheat toast can be traded for one reduced-fat, 4 1/2-inch-square waffle). Your dietitian can help you figure out what your total number of exchanges from all of the groups should be for each day.

Carbohydrate Counting

When using this meal-planning tool, you count the grams of carbohydrate in the foods you eat. You don't count vegetables, meats, or fats. You can find out how much carbohydrate a food has by looking at food labels, the Exchange Lists, or books on carbohydrate counting. As with all meal-planning methods, you still need to pay attention to the total number of calories you're consuming.

Soul Food Pyramid

The Soul Food Pyramid was devised by all of us at Hebni Nutrition Consultants, Inc., to help people work their favorite soul food traditions into a healthy eating plan. It gives you a way to visualize the different types of foods in your meal plan and how much of each you should eat. You'll see the daily number of servings to eat from each food group. The group with the largest number of servings is on the bottom. As you go up the pyramid, you eat more sparingly from the groups. You'll also notice that this revised version of the Soul Food Pyramid puts exercise and water on the two bottom levels. Believe it or not, most people don't drink enough water in a day and everyone should get more exercise. Consider these the first two "food groups" in your healthy eating plan!

fist = 1 cup (Example: 2 servings of pasta or oatmeal)

 palm = 3 oz. (Example: a cooked serving of lean meat)

 thumb tip = 1 teaspoon (Example: 1 tsp. of margarine)

handful = 1 or 2 oz snackfood (Example: 1 oz of nuts = handful; 2 oz pretzels - 2 handfuls)

 thumb = 1 oz (Example: a piece of cheese)

FOOD GROUPS

CALORIES

1600	2000
Many Women & Older Adults	Children, Teens, Active Women and Most Men

Grains, Breads & Cereals
Make 1/2 your grains whole

1 slice of bread, 100% whole wheat, barley, or oat bran bread, 1/2 cup cooked whole grain pasta, 1 cup whole grain cereal, 1/2 cup cooked cream of wheat or oatmeal, 1/2 small bagel, 1/2 hot dog or hamburger bun, 1/2 cup cooked brown rice, grits or macaroni, 1 cup ready to eat flaked cereal (no sugar coating), 1 small piece of cornbread

Grains, Breads & Cereals	
5 servings	6 servings

Vegetables
Choose a variety of vegetables

2 cups raw green vegetables, 1 cup cooked vegetables: collards, mustard greens, turnip greens, callalou, kale, green beans, green cabbage, spinach, small sweet potato, squash, corn, carrots and onions, 1 cup low salt vegetable juice

Vegetables	
2 cup	2-1/2 cup

Fruits
Eat a variety of fruits

Limit juice to 1 cup daily, 100% fruit juice (NOT FRUIT PUNCH), 1 medium: apple, banana, peach, mango, orange, pear, 1/2 grapefruit, 1 cup melon, 1 hand full of grapes, blackberries or strawberries, 1/2 cup canned fruit packed in water or in fruit juice (NO ADDED SUGAR)

Fruits	
1-1/2 cup	2 cup

Milk
Choose low fat calcium rich foods

1 cup of skim or low fat milk, buttermilk, 1 % milk, or lactose reduced milk, 1/2 cup low fat ice cream, or frozen yogurt, 1/2 cup low fat cottage cheese, 1 - 1/2 ounce cheese, cheddar, colby, low fat american, provolone, mozzarella

Milk	
3 cup	3 cup

Meat & Beans
Go lean with protein

Meats & Beans	
5 oz.	5-1/2 oz.

* not including discretionary calories.

5 to 5 - 1/2 ounces for the entire day. Baked, broil, grilled, eat fish at least three times a week. Choose lean beef, lamb, pork, goat, venison, skinless poultry, lean ground beef and turkey, 1/4 cup cooked dry peas and beans, 1 ounce of nuts, 1 tbsp peanut butter, tofu or meat substitutes, 3 egg yolks a week.

> **Solid fats are not recommended**
>
> 1 Tbsp mayonnaise = 100 calories, 10 grams fat
>
> 3 oz. chitterlings = 258 calories, 24 grams fat
>
> 1 tsp. butter = 34 calories, 3.8 grams fat
>
> 1 tsp table salt = 2400 mg sodium
>
> 1 tsp. sugar = 16 calories

Fats & Oils
Limit your fats

Foods such as chitterlings, (Chitlins), fresh pork neck bones, fat back, hog jowls, streak-o-lean, pig feet and sausage are sometimes used as meat by many African Americans. Due to the high fat content, these foods should be used only occasionally and in very small amounts. Canola oil and olive oil are recommended. Limit foods containing high amounts of saturated and trans fatty acids. All fats and oils should be used in moderation.

Sweet & Desserts
Foods we love that don't love us

Snacks and sweets: such as cakes, pies, cookies and other rich desserts should be eaten in moderation. Candies, soft drinks, alcoholic beverages and snack food items, such as chips, cheese puffs, corn chips, and pork skins should not be eaten often because they have large amounts of sugar, fat and salt. Remember 1 tsp of sugar = 16 calories

Nutrition Facts
Serving Size 1 cup (228g)
Servings Per Container 2

Amount Per Serving	
Calories 250	Calories from Fat 110

	% Daily Value*
Total Fat 12g	18%
Saturated Fat 3g	15%
Trans Fat 3g	
Cholesterol 30mg	10%
Sodium 470mg	20%
Total Carbohydrate 31g	10%
Dietary Fiber 0g	0%
Sugars 5g	
Protein 5g	
Vitamin A	4%
Vitamin C	2%
Calcium	20%
Iron	4%

* Percent Daily Values are based on a 2,000 calorie diet. Your Daily Values may be higher or lower depending on your calorie needs.

	Calories:	2,000	2,500
Total Fat	Less than	65g	80g
Sat Fat	Less than	20g	25g
Cholesterol	Less than	300mg	300mg
Sodium	Less than	2,400mg	2,400mg
Total Carbohydrate		300g	375g
Dietary Fiber		25g	30g

① Start Here
② Check Calories
③ Limit these Nutrients
⑥ Quick Guide to %DV
5% or less is Low
20% or more is High
④ Get enough of these Nutrients
⑤ Foot note

If you'd like to read more about the Soul Food Pyramid or order a copy to carry with you at all times, visit the Hebni Nutrition Consultants, Inc., website at http://www.soulfoodpyramid.org.

There Has to Be a Catch

Unfortunately, there is. It's in the portion sizes. You will probably need to learn to eat smaller amounts of the foods you like. The first step to take is to serve yourself smaller portions. To feel full on less, you can try drinking water with your meal, eating more fiber-rich foods, such as salads and whole grains, and exercising.

If you're having trouble losing weight, you may not realize how much you're eating. You might even be shocked to find out! Your dietitian will help you decide how much you should be eating each day. The following guidelines should give you a better idea of appropriate portion sizes.

Food Item	Approximate Measure
3 ounces of meat, poultry, or fish	The palm of your hand, a deck of cards, or a cassette tape
1 cup of potato, pasta, or rice	Your fist or a tennis ball
1 ounce of cheese	A pair of dice or the length of your thumb
1 medium fruit	Your fist

Here are some more tips to control portion size:

- Use smaller plates and dishes, so smaller portions won't look lost on the dish.
- Restrict meals to one location in the house. Eating in front of the TV often causes us to eat more without realizing it.

> Keep all serving dishes in the kitchen, instead of on the table, so you have to think before going back for more.

> Don't measure your food every time you eat. Instead, measure your dishes, bowls, and glasses to get a general idea of how much food or beverage they'll hold. This is one of the easiest ways to control your portions at home.

What Else Will Help?

Reading food labels is a handy way to learn more about what you're eating. Take a look at this food label.

Nutrition Facts

Serving Size 1 cup (228g)
Servings Per Container 2

Amount Per Serving

Calories 260	Calories from Fat 120

	% Daily Value*
Total Fat 13g	**20%**
Saturated Fat 5g	**25%**
Trans Fat 2g	
Cholesterol 30mg	**10%**
Sodium 660mg	**28%**
Total Carbohydrate 31g	**10%**
Dietary Fiber 0g	**0%**
Sugars 5g	
Protein 5g	

Vitamin A 4%	•	Vitamin C 2%
Calcium 15%	•	Iron 4%

* Percent Daily Values are based on a 2,000 calorie diet. Your Daily Values may be higher or lower depending on your calorie needs.

	Calories:	2,000	2,500
Total Fat	Less than	65g	80g
Sat Fat	Less than	20g	25g
Cholesterol	Less than	300mg	300mg
Sodium	Less than	2,400mg	2,400mg
Total Carbohydrate		300g	375mg
Dietary Fiber		25g	30g

Calories per gram:
Fat 9 • Carbohydrate 4 • Protein 4

Serving size

Serving size is one of the most important pieces of information on the food label. You need to make sure that the serving size on your meal plan is the same size as the one on the label. If you eat double the serving size listed, you need to double the listed nutrient and calorie values. If you eat one-half the serving size shown here, cut the nutrient and calorie values in half.

Calories

You may be overweight now, but you can shed that extra weight if you know how many calories you're supposed to eat at each meal and how much each food adds to your daily total. This line on the food label is just as important as serving size.

Total Carbohydrate

About 40–50% of your total daily calories should come from carbohydrate. Carbohydrate-rich foods are breads, potatoes, fruits, and vegetables. Choose these often! They give you valuable nutrients and energy.

Dietary Fiber

Mama always said this would keep you "regular." Fiber is an important part of any diet. Fruits, vegetables, whole-grain foods, beans, and peas are all good sources of fiber and may help reduce the risk of heart disease and cancer.

Protein

Most African Americans get more protein than they need. Only about 10–20% of your total daily calories should come from protein. Eating red meat also means a higher intake of saturated fat and cholesterol. Eat small servings of lean meat, fish, and poultry. Try thinking of meat as a condiment for your vegetables. Use vegetable-protein combinations such as rice and beans instead of fatty roasts or fried foods.

Vitamins and Minerals

Don't count on one food to provide 100% of a nutrient for the day. Instead, let a combination of foods add up to a healthy daily average.

Total Fat

This is the category that gets most of us in trouble. We all need to cut back on fat! Too much fat may contribute to heart disease, diabetes, and cancer. Try to reduce your intake of calories from fat by switching to nonfat or low-fat milk, yogurt, and cheese. For a healthy heart, choose foods with a big difference between the total number of calories and the number of calories from fat.

Saturated Fat

This is not a new kind of fat. We know it as that fat that is visible on the different types of meat we eat. This is listed separately because it's a key player in raising blood cholesterol and increasing your risk of heart disease. Use unsaturated fats such as canola oil and olive oil instead of lard, and trim the fat from your meat before cooking it.

Trans Fat

Trans fats are produced when liquid oil is made into a solid fat using a process called hydrogenation. Trans fats act like saturated fats and can raise your cholesterol level, so they should be avoided. Avoid foods that contain hydrogenated oil or in which a liquid oil is listed first in the ingredient list, which is a sign that the food contains a lot of trans fat. Reducing your trans fat intake is so important that the FDA has required that all food labels display it.

Cholesterol

Too much cholesterol in your diet may contribute to high blood cholesterol levels, which can cause heart attacks, stroke, and high blood pressure. Cut back by using egg substitutes and eating smaller servings of meat, fish, and poultry.

Sodium

We call it "salt," and food labels call it "sodium." Either way, it may add up to high blood pressure in some people. Try using red pepper, herbs, and spices instead of salt to season your soul food favorites.

% Daily Value

Daily values are listed for people who eat 2,000 or 2,500 calories each day. If you eat more, your personal daily value may be higher than what's listed on the label. If you eat less, your personal daily value may be lower. For fat, saturated fat, trans fat, cholesterol, and sodium, choose foods with a low % Daily Value. For dietary fiber, vitamins, and minerals, your Daily Value goal is to reach 100% of each.

What Is Your Eating Style?

How many times have you skipped breakfast because you think it's a good way to cut a few calories from your daily intake? How often have you skipped lunch because you were not hungry and then, later in the day, ate too much because you were so hungry? How many times have you found yourself following some fad diet that didn't work? Do you eat when you're lonely, angry, or depressed? Do you have difficulty resisting high-fat, high-sugar foods at family gatherings or church socials?

If so, take a careful look at your personal eating style. If you don't take a good, honest look at yourself, you will find it harder to practice healthy habits. New habits should be easy to incorporate, as long as you make specific, realistic goals and introduce small changes one at a time. Don't try to change everything at once. Also, find what works for you. We're all different, and what worked for your neighbor, friend, or relative may not suit you.

The Food Diary

One way to examine your personal eating style is to keep a Food Diary. For one week, write down everything you eat, what time you eat, and how you feel before or after eating, and rate how hungry you were on a scale of 1 to 10. If you skip a meal or snack, write down why ("late for work" or "not hungry," for example).

After one week, meet with your dietitian or physician and see what you can learn from the Food Diary. You may find that you skip breakfast on workdays and that you're starving by 11:00 a.m. You may notice that you eat more than you thought late at night while in front of the TV. You may see that you're so hungry by dinnertime that you stop at a fast-food restaurant because it would take too long to cook dinner.

Using this information, decide on one or two changes that you want to make to improve your eating habits. For example, you could decide to wake up 15 minutes earlier and eat some cereal in the morning or take a leisurely walk after dinner instead of eating dessert. Continue updating your Food Diary to document how well you're sticking with these changes.

Be patient with yourself and you'll see progress over time. Once these changes become a habit (usually after 6 weeks or so), decide on a new change and start the process again. Taking these small steps will make long-term goals more easy to achieve.

Here are some suggestions for simple changes you can make in your eating habits that will help you feel better.

- Eat breakfast! When people eat an adequate number of calories earlier in the day, they are less likely to overeat later in the day. Eating most of your food at night is a habit that can add extra calories and eventually increase your weight. Remember, breakfast doesn't have to consist of eggs, grits, sausage, and ham. It could be a turkey sandwich and a glass of juice or just a bowl of healthy cereal.

- You may want to plan a snack, such as a piece of fruit or glass of nonfat milk, for the late afternoon. This will slow down your urge to eat while you're making dinner. You will find that you are eating less each day if you spread out your meals and snacks throughout the day.

- Eat slowly, savor each bite, and remember that your next meal or snack is only a few hours away!

Eating Out

It can be hard to resist your favorite holiday, family, or restaurant foods, especially if you already feel deprived by your new healthy eating goals. The key here is to realize that you can still have almost all of your old favorites—you just need to have less of them and enjoy them less often.

You can avoid feeling overwhelmed by food cravings by using a few small tactics. First, remind yourself that your goal is to stay healthy and well. That particular food and the enjoyment it may offer is not more important than your overall health.

Second, remember that you can have a small portion of those special occasion foods—you just need to account for them in your daily total of calories, exchanges, or carbohydrates. A dietitian can help you figure out how to do this in advance, so you can go to a party or restaurant armed with a plan.

Finally, try to eat a small meal or snack before you go out; that way you don't arrive at the restaurant starving and totally abandon your plan.

When you go out to eat, try these tips.

- Go to restaurants that provide a variety of choices and alternatives.

- Look for lighter fare on the menu or choices marked as lower in fat or calories. These usually have a healthy eating icon next to them.

- Don't be embarrassed to ask the waiter how the food is prepared or what the portion sizes are.

- Ask for sauces and dressings to be served on the side.

- Try eating early-bird specials or appetizers as entrées, both of which usually come in smaller portions.

- Try to avoid feeling like "I paid for it, so I have to eat all of it." Your health is more important than not wasting food.

- Plan your day carefully if you know you are going to have dinner away from home. Make sure you follow the rest of your meal plan.

- Avoid "all-you-can-eat" specials and buffets.

- Look for words and phrases such as baked, braised, broiled, cooked in its own juices, grilled, poached, roasted, steamed, and stir-fried. These cooking methods require less fat and are healthier choices.

- Avoid choices on the menu that include terms such as au gratin, batter-fried, fried, breaded, buttered, sautéed, gravy, white sauce, deep-fried, french-fried, pastry, double crust, scalloped, mayonnaise, hollandaise sauce, pan-fried, rich, thick sauce, creamed, and crispy. These usually indicate high-fat ingredients that will throw your healthy eating plan off its track.

- Plan to have a little of your favorite dessert and work out what adjustments are necessary for the rest of your daily meal plan.

- Eat at a leisurely pace and enjoy the special atmosphere.

- Build nice salads from the salad bar, but watch your choice of and amount of dressings and toppers, such as bacon, croutons, nuts, olives, and cheese.

- Avoid deluxe and super-size items when you go to drive-through restaurants—you'd be surprised by how often less is more than enough.

- Split your order with someone if there is too much food or take your leftovers home and save them for another meal.

What about Salt?

There's no doubt about it: soul food can be salty. It also tastes just as good without the salt, if you make a few simple substitutions. You'd be amazed what spices, peppers, and herbs can do for a soul food recipe. It isn't as hard as you think to retrain your taste buds to survive without salt. Even more, with the great plagues of hypertension, diabetes, and heart disease upon us, it's important that you do.

Sodium and salt are found mainly in processed and prepared foods. Think about the amount of salt in bacon, hot dogs, sausages, canned foods, frozen foods, cheese, pickles, mustard, salad dressing, and snack foods. But if you buy more fresh meats, grains, fruits, and vegetables and prepare them with lemon juice, reduced-fat margarine, pepper, herbs, spices, and smoked seasoning, then you will find that you don't need nearly as much salt. The extra potassium found in fresh fruits and vegetables can also help lower blood pressure.

Most people with high blood pressure need to eat 2,400 mg of sodium or less each day. To help you picture how much that is, 1/4 teaspoon of salt has 450 mg of sodium, 1 ounce of processed American cheese has 400 mg, and 8 ounces of milk has 120 mg. There are plenty of low-sodium varieties of food on the market today to help you eat less salt. Use garlic, onion, and celery powders in place of garlic, onion, and celery salt. Also, use fresh herbs, such as parsley and basil, whenever possible for the best flavor.

Can I Still Make My Favorite Recipes?

To use your favorite recipes in your new meal plan, try one or more of these simple adjustments and substitutions.

Instead of	Use This
Bacon	Turkey bacon or sausage
Butter	Low- or reduced-fat margarine
Cheese	Low- or reduced-fat cheese
Corn chips	Baked tortilla chips
Cream cheese	Fat-free cream cheese
Cream	Evaporated skim milk
Creamy salad dressing	Olive oil and vinegar
Croissants	Bagels or pita bread
Egg yolks	Egg substitute
Fried chicken	Grilled or baked chicken
Fried fish	Baked fish
Fried meats	Baked, roasted, or grilled meats
Ground beef	Lean ground beef
Ground turkey	Ground turkey breast
Ham hocks	Smoked turkey or liquid smoke
Heavy sauces	Light broths
High-fat meats	Trimmed or lean meats
Ice cream	Sherbet or low-fat ice cream

Instead of	Use This
Jelly, jam, or syrups	Fruit spreads
Mayonnaise	Low- or reduced-fat mayonnaise
Pork chops	Pork tenderloin
Potato chips	Pretzels
Salt pork	Smoked turkey
Sour cream	Plain nonfat yogurt or fat-free sour cream
Sugary cereals	Whole-grain cereals
Tuna packed in oil	Tuna packed in water
Vegetable oil, lard	Canola and olive oils or nonstick cooking spray
Whole milk	Nonfat or 1% milk

You can also use different cooking techniques to reduce the fat and calories in your food. For example, skip frying and try baking instead.

Remember, you will feel much better and are more likely to keep your healthy eating plan on track if you keep your goals in mind.

- Maintain a healthy weight
- Eat smaller meals
- Eat on time
- Eat a variety of fresh foods
- Eat sensible portions
- Read food labels

You'll Feel Better if You . . .

There's one more thing you can do to feel great and keep your health under control: exercise. This doesn't mean you have to do anything drastic! The introduction of a simple walking program will do wonders for your health, energy, and state of mind.

What are the health benefits of physical activity? Research consistently shows that regular physical activity, combined with healthy eating habits, is the most efficient and reliable way to control your weight.

Regular physical activity can also help prevent several conditions, including heart disease, diabetes, stroke, high blood pressure, osteoporosis, and back pain. Exercise can improve your mood and the way you feel about yourself, as well as reduce depression and anxiety and help you to better manage stress.

It doesn't matter what type of physical activity you perform—sports, planned exercise, household chores, yard work, or work-related tasks—all are beneficial. Studies show that even the most inactive people can gain significant health benefits if they accumulate 30 minutes or more of physical activity per day.

Keep these tips in mind when developing an exercise program.

- Follow a gradual approach to exercise to get the most benefits with the fewest risks. If you have not been exercising, start at a slow pace. As you become more fit, gradually increase the duration and pace of your activity.

- If you have not exercised in a long time or if you suffer from any kind of condition that may make physical activity dangerous, see your physician beforehand so he or she can help you develop a safe and effective exercise plan.

- Choose activities that you enjoy and that fit your personality. For example, if you like team sports or group activities, choose things such as soccer or aerobics. If you prefer individual activities, choose things such as swimming or walking.

- Plan your activities for a time of day that suits your personality. If you are a morning person, exercise before you begin the rest of your day's activities. If you have more energy in the evening, plan activities that can be done at the end of the day. You will be more likely to stick to a physical activity program if it is convenient and enjoyable.

- Exercise regularly. To gain the most health benefits, it is important to exercise as regularly as possible. Make sure you choose activities that will fit into your schedule.

- Exercise at a comfortable pace. For example, while jogging or walking briskly, you should still be able to have a conversation. If you do not feel normal again within 10 minutes following exercise, you are exercising too hard. Also, if you have difficulty breathing or feel faint or weak during or after exercise, you are exercising too hard.

- Maximize your safety and comfort. Wear shoes that fit and clothes that move with you, and always exercise in a safe location. Many people walk in indoor shopping malls for exercise. Malls are climate controlled and offer protection from bad weather.

- Vary your activities. Choose a variety of activities so you don't get bored with any one thing.

- Encourage your family or friends to support you and join you in your activity. If you have children, it is best to build healthy habits when they are young. When parents are active, children are more likely to be active and stay active for the rest of their lives.

- Challenge yourself. Set short- and long-term goals. Celebrate every success, no matter how small.

What if I Just Want To Start Walking?

Walking is one of the easiest ways to exercise. You can do it almost any-where and anytime. Walking is also inexpensive—the only equipment you need is a pair of comfortable shoes.

Walking will

- give you more energy.
- help you feel good.
- help you relax.
- reduce stress.
- help you sleep better.
- tone your muscles.
- help control your appetite.
- increase the number of calories your body uses.

Answer the following questions before you begin a walking program.

- Has your doctor ever told you that you have heart trouble?
- When you exercise, do you have pains in your chest or on your left side (neck, shoulder, or arm)?
- Do you often feel faint or have dizzy spells?
- Do you feel extremely breathless after mild activity?
- Has your doctor told you that you have high blood pressure?
- Has your doctor told you that you have bone or joint prob-lems, such as arthritis, that could get worse if you exercise?
- Are you middle-aged and not used to a lot of exercise?
- Do you have a condition or physical reason not mentioned here that might interfere with an exercise program?

If you answered yes to any of these questions, please check with your doctor before starting a walking program or other form of exercise.

It is important to design a program that will work for you. In planning your walking program, keep these points in mind.

- Stretch before you walk.

- Wear shoes with thick, flexible soles that will cushion your feet and absorb shock.

- If you have diabetes, your feet and shoes should be inspected after exercising.

- Wear clothes that are right for the season. In the summer, light cotton clothes allow sweat to evaporate, which helps keep you cool. Use layers of clothing in the winter and shed them as you warm up.

- Think of your walk in three parts. Walk slowly for 5 minutes. Increase your speed for the next 5 minutes. Finally, to cool down, walk slowly again for 5 minutes.

- Try to walk at least three times per week, and add 2 to 3 minutes per week to the fast-walk portion of your program. If you walk less than three times per week, increase the fast walk more slowly.

- To avoid stiff or sore muscles or joints, start gradually. Over several weeks, begin walking faster and walking for longer periods of time.

Always keep safety in mind when you plan your route and the time of your walk.

- Walk in the daytime or at night in well-lighted areas.

- Walk with a partner or in a group.

- Avoid wearing jewelry or headphones.

- Be aware of your surroundings.

Here's a sample 9-week walking program that you may enjoy. Be sure to check with your physician before beginning any exercise program.

	Warm Up	Fast Walk	Cool Down	Total Time
Week 1	Slow 5 min	Brisk 5 min	Slow 5 min	15 min
Week 2	Slow 5 min	Brisk 8 min	Slow 5 min	18 min
Week 3	Slow 5 min	Brisk 11 min	Slow 5 min	21 min
Week 4	Slow 5 min	Brisk 14 min	Slow 5 min	24 min
Week 5	Slow 5 min	Brisk 17 min	Slow 5 min	27 min
Week 6	Slow 5 min	Brisk 20 min	Slow 5 min	30 min
Week 7	Slow 5 min	Brisk 23 min	Slow 5 min	33 min
Week 8	Slow 5 min	Brisk 26 min	Slow 5 min	36 min
Week 9 & beyond	Slow 5 min	Brisk 30 min	Slow 5 min	40 min

Combining healthy eating with an easy, fun exercise program will help you feel better and healthier, too.

Mama's Favorite Beef and Pork

Althea's Beef Gumbo

Preparation time: 20 min   Serves 7   Serving size: 1 cup

1	lb lean ground beef
2	large onions, chopped
16	oz frozen white corn kernels, thawed
1	15-oz can navy beans, rinsed and drained
3	14 1/2-oz cans reduced-sodium stewed tomatoes, with juice
1	10-oz pkg frozen sliced okra, thawed
2	Tbsp chili powder
2 1/3	cups cooked rice

1. Brown the ground beef and onion in a large soup pot or Dutch oven, stirring until the beef crumbles. Drain the beef, discarding fat.

2. Stir in the remaining ingredients except for the rice and bring the mixture to a boil over medium heat, stirring occasionally.

3. Cover and reduce the heat; simmer 20 minutes. Stir occasionally. Serve over 1/3 cup rice.

EXCHANGES
3 1/2 Starch
2 Lean Meat

Calories 390
  Calories from Fat 92
Total Fat . . . . 10 g
  Saturated Fat . . . . 3 g
Cholesterol . . . . 41 mg
Sodium . . . . 200 mg
Total Carbohydrate . . . 56 g
  Dietary Fiber . . . . 9 g
  Sugars . . . . 11 g
Protein . . . . 22 g

Baked Pork Hawaiian

2　lb lean boneless pork sirloin roast, trimmed of fat

　　Salt to taste (optional)

　　Pepper to taste (optional)

1/2　cup diced onion

1/4　cup diced green pepper

2　8-oz cans tomato sauce

1　Tbsp Worcestershire sauce

1/3　cup apple cider vinegar

1　8-oz can pineapple tidbits packed in their own juice

1/4　cup brown sugar

1/2　tsp dry mustard

1. Heat the oven to 350°F. Sprinkle the pork with salt and pepper and place in a shallow pan. Bake for 1 hour. Drain off all excess fat.

2. Meanwhile, mix the remaining ingredients together and let stand to blend flavors.

3. Pour the sauce over the pork and bake an additional 45–60 minutes, basting frequently or until thermometer registers 155°F. Remove from oven and cover with aluminum foil. Let rest for 10 minutes. Carve into thin slices.

EXCHANGES
1 Carbohydrate
2 Lean Meat

Calories 177
　Calories from Fat 47
Total Fat . . . . 5 g
　Saturated Fat . . . . 1.8 g
Cholesterol . . . . 53 mg
Sodium . . . . 330 mg
Total Carbohydrate . . . . 14 g
　Dietary Fiber . . . . 1 g
　Sugars . . . . 12 g
Protein . . . . 19 g

Barbecue Pulled Pork

Preparation time: 10 min   Serves 4   Serving size: 4 oz

1	lb boneless pork tenderloin
1/2	tsp pepper
1/4	tsp red pepper flakes
1	Tbsp canola oil
1	cup diced onion
2	cloves garlic, minced
1/2	cup barbecue sauce
1/4	cup catsup
1/4	cup water
1	tsp vinegar

1. Heat the oven to 350°F. Sear the whole tenderloin on all sides in a hot, nonstick skillet. Remove from heat and season with the pepper and red pepper flakes.

2. Cover the tenderloin with foil and bake for 25 minutes. Heat the oil in a medium saucepan and sauté the onion and garlic for 5 minutes.

3. Add the barbecue sauce, catsup, water, and vinegar. Simmer for 10 minutes. Shred the pork with two forks. Add the pulled pork to the sauce. Serve on buns.

EXCHANGES
1 Carbohydrate
3 Lean Meat

Calories 230
  Calories from Fat 76
Total Fat . . . . 8 g
  Saturated Fat . . . . 0 g
Cholesterol . . . . 65 mg
Sodium . . . . 482 mg
Total Carbohydrate . . . . 13 g
  Dietary Fiber . . . . 1 g
  Sugars . . . . 9 g
Protein . . . . 25 g

Bernetha's Pork Chops

Preparation time: 20 min   Serves 4   Serving size: 1 chop

2	tsp sesame oil, divided
12	oz lean boneless pork chops, trimmed of fat
1	tsp minced garlic
1/2	tsp minced ginger
4	Tbsp rice wine
3	Tbsp lite soy sauce
2 1/2	Tbsp brown sugar
	Red pepper flakes (optional)
2	tsp cornstarch
2	Tbsp water

1. Heat 1 tsp oil in a skillet. Brown the pork chops, garlic, and ginger in the oil, turning once.

2. In a small bowl, combine 1 tsp oil, wine, soy sauce (omit this if you need to reduce total sodium), brown sugar, and red pepper flakes. Pour the sauce over the chops and cover tightly. Simmer over low heat until the chops are tender and cooked through, about 15–20 minutes.

3. Mix the cornstarch and water together. Remove the chops from the skillet and add the cornstarch mixture, stirring well. Cook until thickened, about 5 minutes. Pour the sauce over the chops to serve.

EXCHANGES
1/2 Carbohydrate
2 Lean Meat

Calories	157
Calories from Fat	56
Total Fat	6 g
Saturated Fat	1.9 g
Cholesterol	28 mg
Sodium	450 mg
Total Carbohydrate	11 g
Dietary Fiber	0 g
Sugars	9 g
Protein	12 g

Daddy's Favorite Pork Chops

Preparation time: 20 min   Serves 6   Serving size: 1 chop

6	3-oz lean, boneless pork chops
	Salt to taste (optional)
	Pepper to taste (optional)
1	medium onion, chopped
3/4	cup catsup
1	cup water
2	Tbsp Worcestershire sauce
2	Tbsp apple cider vinegar
2	Tbsp brown sugar
1 1/4	tsp paprika
1 1/4	tsp chili powder

1. Heat the oven to 325°F. Season the pork chops with salt and pepper (if desired) and place in a baking dish with a cover. Spread chopped onions evenly over the chops.

2. Combine the remaining ingredients in a small bowl, mix well, and pour over the chops. Cover and bake for 1 1/2 hours. Bake uncovered for the last 20 minutes.

EXCHANGES
1 Carbohydrate
2 Lean Meat

Calories	183
Calories from Fat	53
Total Fat	6 g
Saturated Fat	2.2 g
Cholesterol	38 mg
Sodium	452 mg
Total Carbohydrate	17 g
Dietary Fiber	1 g
Sugars	11 g
Protein	16 g

Easy Beef Casserole

Preparation time: 15 min   Serves 4   Serving size: 4 oz

1	lb extra-lean, boneless top round steak, cut into bite-sized pieces and trimmed of fat
2	cups sliced carrots
1	medium onion, chopped
1/2	cup water
2	Tbsp Worcestershire sauce
1	tsp garlic powder
1	tsp parsley
2	Tbsp red wine
1/2	tsp salt
	Pepper to taste (optional)

1. Heat the oven to 350°F. Place the steak, carrots, and onions in a casserole dish.

2. Combine the remaining ingredients in a small bowl and mix well. Add to beef dish. Cover the dish tightly with aluminum foil and bake for 1 1/2 hours, keeping the dish covered at all times.

EXCHANGES
2 Vegetable
2 Lean Meat

Calories	181
Calories from Fat	31
Total Fat	3 g
Saturated Fat	1.2 g
Cholesterol	59 mg
Sodium	462 mg
Total Carbohydrate	12 g
Dietary Fiber	2 g
Sugars	6 g
Protein	25 g

Marinated Steak

2	lb lean boneless sirloin, about 3/4 inch thick
1	tsp salt
1/4	tsp pepper
1	Tbsp garlic powder, divided
1/2	cup dry red wine
1	tsp parsley
1	tsp oregano
1	tsp olive oil
1/2	cup fresh mushrooms

1. Rub the beef with salt, pepper, and garlic powder. Mix together the wine, parsley, and oregano. Pour over the meat and marinate in the refrigerator for 12 hours, turning often.

2. Remove the steak from the marinade and pat dry with a paper towel. Discard the marinade.

3. Heat the oil in a heavy skillet and sauté the mushrooms on high heat, turning frequently, for 3 minutes. Add the steak and sauté for 4–7 minutes on each side, depending on desired doneness.

EXCHANGES
3 Lean Meat

Calories 148
  Calories from Fat 49
Total Fat . . . . 5 g
  Saturated Fat . . . . 3 g
Cholesterol . . . . 64 mg
Sodium . . . . 340 mg
Total Carbohydrate . . . . 1 g
  Dietary Fiber . . . . 0 g
  Sugars . . . . 0 g
Protein . . . . 22 g

Pork Chops with Fruit Sauce

Preparation time: 15 min   Serves 4   Serving size: 1 chop

2	Tbsp sugar
2	Tbsp cornstarch
1/8	tsp allspice
1	cup water
1/4	cup orange juice
2	Tbsp lemon juice
1/2	cup raisins
1/4	cup flour
1/3	tsp salt
1/4	tsp pepper
4	3-oz lean boneless pork chops
2	tsp canola oil
4	orange slices

1. Combine the sugar, cornstarch, and allspice in a small saucepan. Add the water and cook over low heat until thick, stirring constantly. Stir in the fruit juices and raisins. Remove from heat and set aside.

2. Combine the flour, salt, and pepper. Dredge the pork chops in the flour mixture. Heat the oil in a skillet over medium-high heat, and brown the chops quickly on both sides.

3. Pour the juice mixture over the chops and cover. Reduce heat and simmer for 30 minutes or until the chops are tender. Garnish with orange slices and serve.

EXCHANGES
2 Carbohydrate
2 Lean Meat

Calories 273
  Calories from Fat 72
Total Fat . . . . 8 g
  Saturated Fat . . . . 2.3 g
Cholesterol . . . . 39 mg
Sodium . . . . 220 mg
Total Carbohydrate . . . . 34 g
  Dietary Fiber . . . . 1 g
  Sugars . . . . 21 g
Protein . . . . 17 g

Pork Roast

1/3	cup lite soy sauce
1/2	cup dry sherry
2	cloves garlic, minced
1	Tbsp dry mustard
1	tsp ginger
2	tsp thyme
2	lb lean boneless pork sirloin roast

1. Combine the soy sauce, sherry, garlic, and spices in a plastic locking bag and mix well. Place the pork in the bag and marinate in the refrigerator for 10–12 hours.

2. Heat the oven to 325°F. Remove the pork from the marinade, discard the marinade, and roast the pork for 2 hours. Let the roast rest 15 minutes before slicing.

EXCHANGES
3 Lean Meat

Calories 157
   Calories from Fat 58
Total Fat . . . . 6 g
   Saturated Fat . . . . 2.3 g
Cholesterol . . . . 66 mg
Sodium . . . . 170 mg
Total Carbohydrate . . . . . 1 g
   Dietary Fiber . . . . 0 g
   Sugars . . . . 0 g
Protein . . . . 23 g

Pork Supper in One Pot

Preparation time: 15 min   Serves 4   Serving size: 1/4 recipe

4	3-oz lean boneless pork chops
1	10 3/4-oz can condensed tomato soup
1/2	cup water
2	tsp Worcestershire sauce
1/4	tsp salt
3	medium potatoes, peeled and quartered
4	small carrots, split lengthwise and cut into 2-inch pieces

1. In a large nonstick skillet, brown the pork chops. Pour off any fat and add the remaining ingredients (omit the salt if you need to reduce total sodium).

2. Cover the chops and vegetables and cook over low heat for 30–45 minutes or until tender.

EXCHANGES
2 Starch
1 Vegetable
2 Lean Meat

Calories 298
   Calories from Fat 62
Total Fat . . . . 7 g
   Saturated Fat . . . . 2.4 g
Cholesterol . . . . 39 mg
Sodium . . . . 666 mg
Total Carbohydrate . . . . 39 g
   Dietary Fiber . . . . 5 g
   Sugars . . . . 11 g
Protein . . . . 19 g

Pork Tenderloin in Hoisin Sauce

Preparation time: 10 min   Serves 6   Serving size: 4 oz

1/4   cup lite soy sauce
2   Tbsp canola oil
1   Tbsp brown sugar
1/4   cup hoisin sauce
1 1/2   lb lean boneless pork tenderloin
2   cups cooked rice
4   stalks green onion, chopped

1. Mix the soy sauce, canola oil, brown sugar, and hoisin sauce in a plastic locking bag. Add the pork and marinate in the refrigerator for at least 1 hour or overnight.

2. Heat the oven to 350°F. Remove the pork from the marinade and roast it for 15 minutes on each side or until done. Let the pork rest before slicing. Serve with 1/3 cup rice and garnish with green onion.

EXCHANGES
1 Starch
4 Very Lean Meat

Calories 232
 Calories from Fat 52
Total Fat . . . . 6 g
 Saturated Fat . . . . 0 g
Cholesterol . . . . 65 mg
Sodium . . . . 252 mg
Total Carbohydrate . . . . 18 g
 Dietary Fiber . . . . 1 g
 Sugars . . . . 2 g
Protein . . . . 25 g

Quick Beef Stroganoff

1 1/2	lb 96% extra-lean ground beef
1	Tbsp reduced-fat margarine
3/4	cup chopped onion
1/4	cup chopped green bell pepper
1/3	cup flour
1	tsp salt
1/8	tsp garlic powder
1/4	tsp pepper
1	Tbsp Worcestershire sauce
1	6-oz can tomato paste
1	10-oz can beef broth
1	cup fat-free (skim) evaporated milk

1. Brown the ground beef in a heavy skillet. Drain off the fat, remove the beef from the skillet, and set aside. Add the margarine and sauté the onion and bell pepper until tender.

2. Add the remaining ingredients slowly, stirring to blend. Return beef to skillet; stir to coat well. Cover and cook over low heat for 30 minutes. Serve over hot noodles or fluffy rice.

EXCHANGES
1 Carbohydrate
2 Lean Meat

Calories 168
   Calories from Fat 42
Total Fat . . . . 5 g
   Saturated Fat . . . . 1.8 g
Cholesterol . . . . 46 mg
Sodium . . . . 533 mg
Total Carbohydrate . . . . 12 g
   Dietary Fiber . . . . 1 g
   Sugars . . . . 4 g
Protein . . . . 19 g

Roast Beef, Jamaican Style

Preparation time: 20 min   Serves 8   Serving size: 3 oz

1	medium onion, finely chopped
3	stalks green onion, finely chopped
4	garlic cloves, finely chopped
1/2	tsp salt
1 1/2	tsp pepper
2	tsp thyme
2	tsp pimiento seeds (or whole allspice)
2	tsp lite soy sauce
1	Tbsp peppercorns
1 1/2	lb lean boneless eye round beef roast, trimmed of fat
1	Tbsp olive oil

1. Mix all ingredients except the beef and the oil in a small bowl. Wash and dry the beef.

2. Using a thin, sharp knife, puncture the beef on all sides. Open the puncture 1 to 1 1/2 inches deep on all sides. Using your index finger, open the puncture sites and put in the seasoning.

3. Marinate in the refrigerator 12–24 hours. Heat the oven to 300°F. Place the beef in a nonstick baking dish. Rub the oil on the beef and bake for 45 minutes or until done.

EXCHANGES
1 Vegetable
2 Lean Meat

Calories 135
   Calories from Fat 40
Total Fat . . . . 4 g
   Saturated Fat . . . . 1.2 g
Cholesterol . . . . 36 mg
Sodium . . . . 220 mg
Total Carbohydrate . . . . . 4 g
   Dietary Fiber . . . . 1 g
   Sugars . . . . 1 g
Protein . . . . 20 g

Roniece's Jerk Pork Tenderloin

Preparation time: 10 min   Serves 8   Serving size: 4 oz

1/2	cup lite soy sauce
2	tsp thyme
1	tsp oregano
2	Tbsp wet jerk marinade (check the gourmet aisle of your supermarket)
2	lb lean boneless pork tenderloin

1. Place the soy sauce, thyme, oregano, and jerk marinade in a plastic locking bag and mix well. Put the pork in the bag and marinate in the refrigerator for several hours.

2. Remove the pork from the bag and discard the marinade. Grill outside until the pork is well done. To achieve the best results, place the meat away from the hot coals and allow the heat to smoke the pork tenderloin. You may also broil the pork.
Slice into 1/2-inch slices when done.

EXCHANGES
4 Very Lean Meat

Calories	138
Calories from Fat	37
Total Fat	4 g
Saturated Fat	0 g
Cholesterol	65 mg
Sodium	225 mg
Total Carbohydrate	1 g
Dietary Fiber	0 g
Sugars	1 g
Protein	24 g

Smothered Pork Chops

Preparation time: 20 min   Serves 6   Serving size: 3 oz

2	Tbsp flour
1/2	tsp Cajun seasoning
	Salt to taste (optional)
	Pepper to taste (optional)
6	3-oz lean boneless pork chops
1	Tbsp canola oil
1	10-oz bag frozen onion
1	clove garlic, minced
1	10-oz bag frozen green bell pepper
1	10-oz bag frozen celery
1	15-oz can stewed tomatoes
2	bay leaves
1/2	cup water
1/2	tsp oregano
1/2	tsp thyme

1. Mix the flour with the Cajun seasoning, salt, and pepper in a plastic locking bag. Add the pork chops and toss to coat.

2. Heat the oil in a large skillet and brown the chops on both sides. Remove the chops from the skillet and sauté the onion, garlic, bell pepper, and celery for 10 minutes.

3. Add the remaining ingredients to the skillet and mix well. Return the pork chops to the skillet and simmer until tender.

EXCHANGES
3 Vegetable
2 Lean Meat

Calories 199
   Calories from Fat 72
Total Fat . . . . 8 g
   Saturated Fat . . . . 2.3 g
Cholesterol . . . . 38 mg
Sodium . . . . 285 mg
Total Carbohydrate . . . . 14 g
   Dietary Fiber . . . . 3 g
   Sugars . . . . 7 g
Protein . . . . 17 g

Stew Beef with Vegetables

Preparation time: 20 min   Serves 8   Serving size: 4 oz

2	lb lean stew beef, diced
1	10-oz can low-fat cream of mushroom soup
2	cups chopped onions
2	cups sliced carrots
1	cup chopped green bell pepper
2	reduced-sodium beef bouillon cubes
1/2	cup red wine
2	cups water
4	cups cooked rice

1. Combine all ingredients except the rice in a large soup pot. Bring to a boil and reduce the heat.

2. Simmer until the beef becomes tender, about 1 to 1 1/2 hours. Add more water if necessary. Serve over 1/2 cup of hot rice.

EXCHANGES
2 Starch
2 Vegetable
2 Lean Meat

Calories 313
　Calories from Fat 43
Total Fat . . . . 5 g
　Saturated Fat . . . . 0 g
Cholesterol . . . . 64 mg
Sodium . . . . 485 mg
Total Carbohydrate . . . . 35 g
　Dietary Fiber . . . . 2 g
　Sugars . . . . 5 g
Protein . . . . 30 g

Vegetable Beef Skillet

Preparation time: 15 min   Serves 6   Serving size: 1 cup

1/2	lb lean ground beef
1	large onion, sliced
1	cup frozen lima beans, thawed
1	cup frozen green beans, thawed
1	cup frozen corn kernels, thawed
1	tsp garlic salt
1/2	tsp pepper
4	medium tomatoes, peeled and cubed

1. Brown the ground beef in a large skillet, stirring to crumble. Drain off any fat. Add all ingredients except the tomatoes.

2. Cover and cook over low heat for 20 minutes. Add the tomatoes and cook for 5 – 10 minutes more. Serve over steamed rice or noodles.

EXCHANGES
1/2 Starch
2 Vegetable
1 Medium-Fat Meat

Calories 162
   Calories from Fat 52
Total Fat . . . . 6 g
   Saturated Fat . . . . 2 g
Cholesterol . . . . 24 mg
Sodium . . . . 242 mg
Total Carbohydrate . . . . 19 g
   Dietary Fiber . . . . 4 g
   Sugars . . . . 6 g
Protein . . . . 11 g

Mama's Favorite Chicken and Turkey

Asian Lemon Chicken

Preparation time: 20 min   Serves 4   Serving size: 3–4 oz

2	lemons
2	Tbsp canola oil
4	boneless, skinless chicken breast halves, cut into strips
1/2	tsp salt
1/8	tsp pepper
1	cup sliced mushrooms
1/2	green bell pepper, seeded, cut into 1/4-inch strips
1/2	red bell pepper, seeded, cut into 1/4-inch strips
1/2	cup sliced green onion
1/2	tsp grated ginger root
1/2	cup reduced-sodium, reduced-fat chicken broth
2	Tbsp dry sherry
2	Tbsp lite soy sauce
2	tsp cornstarch
1 1/2	tsp sugar

1. Peel 1 lemon; cut the rind into 1/8-inch pieces. Set aside 2 Tbsp of rind. Squeeze both lemons to yield 3 Tbsp of juice; set aside.

2. Pour the oil around the top of a wok or large skillet. Heat the oil for 2 minutes. Sprinkle the chicken with salt (omit this if you want less sodium) and pepper and add it to the wok or skillet. Stir-fry for 2 minutes. Remove the chicken and keep it warm. Add the mushrooms, 2 Tbsp lemon rind, bell pepper, green onion, and ginger root. Stir-fry for 1 minute.

3. Combine 3 Tbsp of lemon juice, chicken broth, sherry, soy sauce, cornstarch, and sugar in a small bowl and mix well. Add the mixture to the wok and stir-fry 3 minutes or until the mixture is thickened. Return the chicken to the wok and stir-fry 1 minute. Serve with steamed rice.

EXCHANGES
1/2 Carbohydrate
4 Lean Meat

Calories	248
Calories from Fat	92
Total Fat	10 g
Saturated Fat	0 g
Cholesterol	72 mg
Sodium	740 mg
Total Carbohydrate	10 g
Dietary Fiber	2 g
Sugars	5 g
Protein	28 g

Chicken and Dumplings

Preparation time: 25 min   Serves 8   Serving size: 1/8 recipe

3	lb chicken fryer, skin removed
1	medium onion, chopped
2	garlic cloves, chopped
2	celery stalks, chopped
4	medium carrots
1	bay leaf
1	reduced-sodium chicken bouillon cube
1/2	tsp salt, divided
1/4	tsp pepper
3	cups flour
1/4	cup egg substitute

1. Cut the chicken into pieces, rinse them, and place in a large pot. Cover with water and add the vegetables, garlic, bay leaf, and bouillon cube. Cook for 1 hour or until tender. Stir in 1/4 tsp salt and the pepper. Remove 1 cup of broth and let cool.

2. Place the flour and remaining 1/4 tsp salt in a mixing bowl. Pour the egg substitute and reserved chicken broth in the center of the bowl. Mix until a soft dough is formed. Roll the dough on a floured surface until thin. Cut the dough into strips and let it stand for 10 minutes.

3. Meanwhile, debone the chicken and bring the broth to a boil. Then drop the strips of dough into the broth. Add the chicken and continue to cook for an additional 15 minutes.

EXCHANGES
3 Starch
2 Very Lean Meat

Calories 311
   Calories from Fat 40
Total Fat . . . . 4 g
   Saturated Fat . . . . 2 g
Cholesterol . . . . 47 mg
Sodium . . . . 318 mg
Total Carbohydrate . . . . 44 g
   Dietary Fiber . . . . 3 g
   Sugars . . . . 4 g
Protein . . . . 22 g

Chicken Fricassee with Rice

Preparation time: 20 min   Serves 8   Serving size: 1/8 recipe

3	lb chicken fryer, skin removed
3/4	cup flour
2	tsp garlic powder
2	Tbsp chili powder
1	tsp thyme
1	tsp oregano
1/2	tsp salt
1/2	tsp pepper
3	Tbsp canola oil
1	medium onion, chopped
1	cup green bell pepper, seeded and chopped
1	cup uncooked rice
1	cup canned tomatoes, undrained
2 1/2	cups boiling water

1. Cut chicken into serving pieces, rinse, and pat dry. In a small bowl, combine the flour, garlic powder, chili powder, thyme, oregano, salt, and pepper. Dredge each chicken piece in the seasoned flour.

2. Heat the oil in a large soup pot. Set the water to boil in a separate pot. Brown the chicken on both sides. Add the onion and bell pepper and stir.

3. Add the rice, tomatoes, and water. Cover and cook until the rice is done.

EXCHANGES

2 Starch
2 Lean Meat
1/2 Fat

Calories 304
   Calories from Fat 90
Total Fat . . . . 10 g
   Saturated Fat . . . . 2 g
Cholesterol . . . . 48 mg
Sodium . . . . 258 mg
Total Carbohydrate . . . . 33 g
   Dietary Fiber . . . . 2 g
   Sugars . . . . 3 g
Protein . . . . 20 g

Chicken Spaghetti

Preparation time: 35 min   Serves 6   Serving size: 1 cup

1/4	cup canola oil, divided
1	green bell pepper, seeded and chopped
1	cup diced celery
2	large onions, chopped
3	cloves garlic, chopped
1	16-oz can tomato purée
2	6-oz cans tomato paste
4	cups water
3	large boneless, skinless chicken breast halves, cut into bite-sized pieces
1	tsp cinnamon
1/2	tsp salt
1/2	tsp pepper
1/2	tsp allspice
8	oz uncooked spaghetti

1. Heat 2 Tbsp oil in a large soup pot. Sauté the green pepper, celery, onions, and garlic in the oil until tender. Add the tomato purée, tomato paste, and water. Simmer uncovered for 1 1/2 hours. Stir often.

2. In a separate skillet, brown the chicken pieces in the remaining 2 Tbsp oil. Add the chicken, cinnamon, salt, pepper, and allspice to the sauce. Continue to simmer, covered, for 1 1/2 hours more or until the chicken is tender.

3. Cook the spaghetti according to package directions, omitting the salt, and drain. Place in a serving dish. Pour the chicken sauce over the spaghetti and serve.

EXCHANGES
4 Starch
2 Lean Meat

Calories 424
    Calories from Fat 111
Total Fat . . . . 12 g
    Saturated Fat . . . . 0 g
Cholesterol . . . . 36 mg
Sodium . . . . 427 mg
Total Carbohydrate . . . . 58 g
    Dietary Fiber . . . . 7 g
    Sugars . . . . 13 g
Protein . . . . 23 g

Country-Fried Chicken

Preparation time: 20 min   Serves 6   Serving size: 1 steak

1	lb boneless, skinless chicken breasts (or turkey breast cutlets)
	Salt to taste (optional)
	Pepper to taste (optional)
1	Tbsp olive oil
2	medium onions, chopped
1	green bell pepper, seeded and chopped
1	clove garlic, chopped
2	Tbsp flour
1/2	tsp gravy browning sauce (such as Kitchen Bouquet)
1/2	cup water
1	cup stewed tomatoes

1. Season the chicken (or turkey) with salt and pepper.

2. Heat the oil in a large skillet and sauté the chicken (or turkey) for 2–3 minutes per side until done. Remove and keep warm under foil. Cook the onion, green pepper, and garlic for 5 minutes. Stir in flour and enough gravy browning sauce (such as Kitchen Bouquet) to make the gravy a desired color.

3. Add water and stir as the gravy thickens. Add stewed tomatoes. Cook until gravy is of desired consistency and serve over chicken (or turkey). Or, if desired, return the chicken (or turkey) to the skillet to heat thoroughly and then serve.

EXCHANGES
2 Vegetable
2 Very Lean Meat
1/2 Fat

Calories 154
    Calories from Fat 38
Total Fat . . . . 4 g
    Saturated Fat . . . . 0.9 g
Cholesterol . . . . 44 mg
Sodium . . . . 150 mg
Total Carbohydrate . . . . 11 g
    Dietary Fiber . . . . 2 g
    Sugars . . . . 4 g
Protein . . . . 17 g

Eunice's Curried Chicken

Preparation time: 20 min   Serves 6   Serving size: 1/6 recipe

3	bone-in chicken breast halves, skin removed
1	tsp salt
2	tsp chives
3	tsp thyme
1	Tbsp canola oil
1	medium onion, chopped
2	cloves garlic, minced
1	Tbsp curry powder
1/2	cup water
1	medium apple, peeled and diced

1. Cut the chicken into six serving pieces, rinse, and pat dry. Combine the salt, chives, and thyme in a small bowl. Roll the chicken in the seasoning.

2. Heat the oil in a large saucepan. Add the chicken pieces and brown for 5 minutes on each side; remove chicken. Add the onion and garlic and cook for 5–7 minutes, stirring occasionally.

3. Mix the curry powder with the water and add it to the skillet. Return chicken to skillet, meaty side down. Stir in the apple and enough water to cover the chicken. Cover and simmer until the chicken is tender, about 15–20 minutes.

EXCHANGES
1/2 Carbohydrate
2 Very Lean Meat
1/2 Fat

Calories 129
  Calories from Fat 38
Total Fat . . . . 4 g
  Saturated Fat . . . . 0.7 g
Cholesterol . . . . 42 mg
Sodium . . . . 426 mg
Total Carbohydrate . . . . . 7 g
  Dietary Fiber . . . . 1 g
  Sugars . . . . 4 g
Protein . . . . 16 g

Honey-Mustard Chicken

Preparation time: 20 min   Serves 4   Serving size: 4 oz

1/4	cup lemon juice
2	Tbsp Dijon mustard
2	Tbsp honey
1	tsp ginger
1	tsp rosemary
4	4-oz boneless, skinless chicken breast halves (about 1 lb total)
1/2	cup dried bread crumbs

1. Combine the lemon juice, mustard, honey, ginger, and rosemary in a small bowl. Place the chicken between sheets of waxed paper and pound to equal thickness.

2. Pour half of the honey-mustard sauce over the chicken. Cover and refrigerate for 20 minutes.

3. Set the oven to broil. Sprinkle the bread crumbs over the top of the chicken and broil for 7–8 minutes. In a saucepan, warm the rest of the sauce and serve with the chicken.

EXCHANGES
1 1/2 Carbohydrate
3 Very Lean Meat

Calories 226
    Calories from Fat 34
Total Fat . . . . 4 g
    Saturated Fat . . . . 1 g
Cholesterol . . . . 66 mg
Sodium . . . . 339 mg
Total Carbohydrate . . . . 21 g
    Dietary Fiber . . . . 1 g
    Sugars . . . . 10 g
Protein . . . . 26 g

Lemon-Lime Chicken

Preparation time: 15 min   Serves 6   Serving size: 1/6 recipe

3	large bone-in chicken breast halves (about 7 oz each), skin removed
1/4	cup lime juice
1/4	cup lemon juice
1/3	cup dry white wine
1	clove garlic, crushed
1	tsp thyme
1	tsp salt
1/8	tsp pepper
	Nonstick cooking spray

1. Cut each chicken breast half into two pieces, rinse, and pat dry. Place the chicken in a bowl or plastic bag. Combine the remaining ingredients and pour over the chicken. Marinate for 2 or more hours in the refrigerator.

2. Heat the oven to 350°F. Spray a baking pan with nonstick cooking spray. Arrange the chicken pieces in the pan and bake for 30–40 minutes or until done.

EXCHANGES

2 Very Lean Meat

Calories 83
Calories from Fat 16
Total Fat . . . . 2 g
Saturated Fat . . . . 0.5 g
Cholesterol . . . . 42 mg
Sodium . . . . 134 mg
Total Carbohydrate . . . . . 0 g
Dietary Fiber . . . . 0 g
Sugars . . . . 0 g
Protein . . . . 15 g

Mary Alice's Chicken and Rice

Preparation time: 20 min   Serves 6   Serving size: 1/6 recipe

4	cups boiling water
1 1/2	lb chicken thighs, skin removed
2	cups uncooked rice
1	medium green bell pepper, seeded and quartered
1	medium onion, chopped
2	bay leaves
1/2	tsp salt
1	tsp pepper
1	tsp garlic powder

1. Add the chicken to the boiling water and cook for 20 minutes. Heat the oven to 350°F.

2. Stir all ingredients together, including the chicken and water, in a large baking pan. Bake for 30 minutes or until the rice is done. Remove the bay leaves to serve.

EXCHANGES
3 1/2 Starch
1 Very Lean Meat

Calories 312
   Calories from Fat 37
Total Fat . . . . 4 g
   Saturated Fat . . . . 1 g
Cholesterol . . . . 32 mg
Sodium . . . . 225 mg
Total Carbohydrate . . . . 53 g
   Dietary Fiber . . . . 1 g
   Sugars . . . . 2 g
Protein . . . . 14 g

Quick Chicken Creole

Preparation time: 20 min   Serves 8   Serving size: 1/8 recipe

1	Tbsp canola oil
4	medium boneless, skinless chicken breast halves, cut into strips
1	14-oz can tomatoes, undrained
1	8-oz can tomato sauce
1 1/2	cups chopped green bell pepper
1/2	cup chopped celery
1/2	cup chopped onion
2	cloves garlic, minced
1/4	tsp salt
1	Tbsp basil
1	Tbsp parsley
1/4	tsp red pepper
2 2/3	cups steamed rice

1. Heat the oil in a large skillet and sauté the chicken about 5 minutes on each side.

2. Add the remaining ingredients and simmer for 20 minutes. Serve over 1/3 cup steamed rice.

EXCHANGES
1 Starch
1 Vegetable
2 Very Lean Meat

Calories 190
   Calories from Fat 32
Total Fat . . . . 4 g
   Saturated Fat . . . . 0 g
Cholesterol . . . . 36 mg
Sodium . . . . 373 mg
Total Carbohydrate . . . . 23 g
   Dietary Fiber . . . . 2 g
   Sugars . . . . 4 g
Protein . . . . 16 g

Rojean's Cornish Hens

Preparation time: 20 min   Serves 8   Serving size: 1/4 hen

2	2-lb Cornish game hens, insides removed
1/2	tsp salt
1/2	tsp pepper
1/2	tsp garlic powder
	Dash paprika
1	Tbsp canola oil
1	medium onion, cut in 4 sections
1	celery stalk, cut in 4 sections
3/4	tsp thyme
1	bay leaf
1	cup Madeira wine
2	tsp chicken bouillon granules
1	cup hot water
1 1/2	Tbsp cornstarch
1	tsp sugar

1. Wash and dry the hens and heat the oven to 425°F. Sprinkle the hens with seasonings and rub with oil inside and out. Place a small piece of onion and celery in each hen. Roast uncovered for 1 hour.

2. Meanwhile, in a small bowl, combine the thyme, bay leaf, and wine; set aside. Dissolve the bouillon in the hot water. Mix in the cornstarch and sugar. Set aside.

3. When the hens are done, remove them to a heated plate and keep them warm. Cut each hen into four servings and remove the skin.

4. Stir the cornstarch mixture into a saucepan and bring to a boil. Reduce the heat. Stir in the wine and simmer for 5 minutes or until thickened. Serve with the hens.

EXCHANGES
1/2 Carbohydrate
3 Very Lean Meat
1 Fat

Calories	172
Calories from Fat	47
Total Fat	5 g
Saturated Fat	1 g
Cholesterol	95 mg
Sodium	433 mg
Total Carbohydrate	6 g
Dietary Fiber	0 g
Sugars	3 g
Protein	21 g

Stewed Chicken

Preparation time: 20 min   Serves 8   Serving size: 1 drumstick

8	chicken drumsticks, skin removed
1	tsp salt
1	tsp pepper
1	tsp thyme
1	tsp sage
1	tsp celery seeds
1	Tbsp olive oil
1	medium onion, chopped
1	clove garlic, chopped
1/3	cup flour
4	cups reduced-sodium, fat-free chicken broth

1. Season the chicken with the salt (omit this if you need to reduce total sodium), pepper, thyme, sage, and celery seeds.

2. Heat the oil in a large skillet. Add the onion and garlic and sauté for 2 minutes. Add the chicken and brown on both sides. Remove the chicken from the skillet.

3. Make a paste out of the flour and broth. Add the paste to the pan drippings. Stir until thick. Return the chicken to the skillet and mix well. Cook for 30 minutes or until the chicken is tender.

EXCHANGES

1/2 Carbohydrate
2 Lean Meat

Calories 147
  Calories from Fat 45
Total Fat . . . . 5 g
  Saturated Fat . . . . 1 g
Cholesterol . . . . 51 mg
Sodium . . . . 594 mg
Total Carbohydrate . . . . . 7 g
  Dietary Fiber . . . . 1 g
  Sugars . . . . 1 g
Protein . . . . 18 g

Sunshine State
Chicken à la Orange

Preparation time: 20 min   Serves 4   Serving size: 4 oz

1	cup chopped tangerine or orange
1/4	cup pineapple juice
1/8	tsp ground mace
1/8	tsp ginger
1/8	tsp red pepper flakes
4	boneless, skinless chicken breast halves
1	cup orange sections
1/2	cup pineapple cubes
1/2	cup sliced strawberries

1. Place the chopped oranges, juice, and spices in a blender or food processor. Blend or process until liquefied. Pour over the chicken and refrigerate for 30 minutes.

2. Heat the oven to broil. Remove the chicken from the marinade and discard the marinade. Broil or grill the chicken for 5 minutes per side or until the chicken juices run clear.

3. Meanwhile, mix the fruit together in a small bowl. Top the chicken with the fruit and serve.

EXCHANGES
1 Fruit
4 Very Lean Meat

Calories 185
   Calories from Fat 29
Total Fat . . . . 3 g
   Saturated Fat . . . . 0 g
Cholesterol . . . . 72 mg
Sodium . . . . 63 mg
Total Carbohydrate . . . . 11 g
   Dietary Fiber . . . . 2 g
   Sugars . . . . 8 g
Protein . . . . 27 g

Tramaine's Oven-Fried Chicken

Preparation time: 15 min   Serves 6   Serving size: 1/6 recipe

3	split chicken breasts with ribs, cut in half and skin removed, or 6 chicken drumsticks, skin removed
1	cup nonfat milk
1	Tbsp reduced-fat margarine
1	tsp thyme
1	tsp garlic powder
1	tsp onion powder
1	tsp parsley
1	tsp paprika
1	tsp pepper
1/2	tsp salt
1/8	tsp red pepper
1	cup flour

1. Place the chicken pieces in the milk. Heat the oven to 400°F. Melt margarine; set aside.

2. In a large bowl, combine all remaining ingredients. Dredge each chicken piece in the flour mixture, making sure all pieces are well coated. Discard remaining flour mixture.

3. Place the chicken in a shallow baking pan and drizzle the top of the chicken with the margarine. Bake for 45 minutes or until the chicken juices run clear.

EXCHANGES
1/2 Carbohydrate
2 Very Lean Meat

Calories 111
    Calories from Fat 23
Total Fat . . . . 3 g
    Saturated Fat . . . . 0.6 g
Cholesterol . . . . 42 mg
Sodium . . . . 103 mg
Total Carbohydrate . . . . . 5 g
    Dietary Fiber . . . . 0 g
    Sugars . . . . 1 g
Protein . . . . 16 g

Turkey Sausage Breakfast Patties

Preparation time: 15 min   Serves 12   Serving size: 2 patties

2 1/2	tsp	sage
1/4	tsp	salt
1	tsp	pepper
3/4	tsp	marjoram
1/4	tsp	allspice
1/4	tsp	nutmeg
1/2	tsp	dry mustard
1	tsp	crushed red pepper flakes
1/4	cup	warm water
1 1/2	lb	lean ground turkey breast

1. Mix the spices together with the warm water. Add to the meat and mix thoroughly. Refrigerate up to 12 hours to develop the flavor.

2. Shape the meat into 24 patties and fry on each side in a nonstick skillet until done, about 7–8 minutes total.

EXCHANGES

2 Very Lean Meat

Calories 66
  Calories from Fat 12
Total Fat . . . . 1 g
  Saturated Fat . . . . 0 g
Cholesterol . . . . 30 mg
Sodium . . . . 75 mg
Total Carbohydrate . . . . . 0 g
  Dietary Fiber . . . . 0 g
  Sugars . . . . 0 g
Protein . . . . 13 g

Turkey Sloppy Joes

Preparation time: 20 min   Serves 4   Serving size: 1/2 cup

       2   tsp canola oil
       1   cup chopped onions
       1   cup chopped green bell pepper
       1   lb lean ground turkey breast
       1   cup tomato sauce
       1   tsp brown sugar
     1/2   cup catsup
       1   tsp red pepper flakes
       2   tsp wine vinegar
     1/4   tsp pepper

1. Heat the oil in a large skillet and sauté the onion and bell pepper until translucent. Add the turkey and cook about 5 minutes. Drain off any fat.

2. Add the remaining ingredients and mix well. Simmer 15 minutes and serve on buns.

3. To reduce the sodium content of this recipe, use salt-free tomato sauce.

EXCHANGES
1/2 Carbohydrate
2 Vegetable
3 Very Lean Meat

Calories 200
  Calories from Fat 29
Total Fat . . . . 3 g
  Saturated Fat . . . . 0.4 g
Cholesterol . . . . 61 mg
Sodium . . . . 766 mg
Total Carbohydrate . . . . 20 g
  Dietary Fiber . . . . 3 g
  Sugars . . . . 10 g
Protein . . . . 24 g

Willa's Lasagna

2	tsp canola oil
1	clove garlic, minced
2	medium onions, chopped
3/4	cup chopped celery
1	green bell pepper, seeded and chopped
1	lb ground breast of turkey
1	6-oz can tomato paste
1	cup water
1/2	cup chopped tomatoes
4	tsp oregano
2	tsp basil
1/2	tsp salt
1/2	tsp pepper
	Nonstick cooking spray
6	lasagna noodle strips, cooked and drained
2	cups 1% (or fat-free) cottage cheese
1 3/4	cups reduced-fat mozzarella cheese

1. Heat the oil in a large skillet and sauté the garlic, onion, celery, bell pepper, and meat. Drain off any fat. Add the tomato paste, water, tomatoes, and seasonings.

2. Cover and simmer for 1 1/2 to 2 hours. Heat the oven to 350°F. In a 2-quart, rectangular baking dish sprayed with nonstick cooking spray, make a layer of noodles, cottage cheese, sauce, and mozzarella cheese. Repeat to make two layers. Bake for 45 minutes.

EXCHANGES
1/2 Starch
2 Vegetable
2 Lean Meat

Calories 215
  Calories from Fat 44
Total Fat . . . . 5 g
  Saturated Fat . . . . 2.2 g
Cholesterol . . . . 37 mg
Sodium . . . . 475 mg
Total Carbohydrate . . . . 20 g
  Dietary Fiber . . . . 2 g
  Sugars . . . . 5 g
Protein . . . . 23 g

Mama's Favorite Seafood

Baked Flounder au Gratin

Preparation time: 15 min   Serves 4   Serving size: 3 oz

1	large flounder (about 2 lb)
	Salt to taste (optional)
	Juice of 1 lemon
1/4	cup dried bread crumbs
1/4	cup shredded reduced-fat cheddar cheese
3	Tbsp reduced-fat margarine
1/2	cup minced onion

1. Have your fish dealer dress the fish for you, which means removing the scales, insides, head, and tail.

2. Heat the oven to 375°F. Sprinkle the fish with salt and lemon juice. Lay fish in shallow nonstick baking dish.

3. Cover with bread crumbs, cheese, small lumps of margarine, and onion. Bake for 35–45 minutes or until fish flakes easily when tested with a fork. Baste the fish from time to time with the pan juices.

EXCHANGES
1/2 Starch
3 Very Lean Meat
1/2 Fat

Calories	167
Calories from Fat	55
Total Fat	6 g
Saturated Fat	1 g
Cholesterol	48 mg
Sodium	254 mg
Total Carbohydrate	8 g
Dietary Fiber	1 g
Sugars	2 g
Protein	19 g

Crabmeat au Gratin

Preparation time: 15 min   Serves 6   Serving size: 1/2 cup

2 Tbsp reduced-fat margarine

1/2 green bell pepper, seeded and minced

1/2 medium onion, chopped

3 Tbsp flour

2 cups nonfat milk

2 cups crabmeat, flaked and shell pieces removed

1/4 tsp salt

Dash nutmeg

1/2 cup shredded reduced-fat cheddar cheese

1/4 cup dried bread crumbs

1. Heat the oven to 350°F. Melt the margarine in a large skillet and sauté the bell pepper and onion for 2 minutes.

2. Add the flour, milk, crabmeat, salt, and nutmeg. Cook for 10 minutes.

3. Pour the crabmeat into a shallow nonstick baking dish. Sprinkle with shredded cheese and bread crumbs. Bake until the cheese browns, about 20 minutes.

EXCHANGES
1 Starch
2 Very Lean Meat

Calories 154
    Calories from Fat 45
Total Fat . . . . 5 g
    Saturated Fat . . . . 2 g
Cholesterol . . . . 45 mg
Sodium . . . . 390 mg
Total Carbohydrate . . . . 12 g
    Dietary Fiber . . . . 1 g
    Sugars . . . . 5 g
Protein . . . . 15 g

Crabmeat Delights

1	Tbsp reduced-fat margarine
8	mushrooms, sliced
1	Tbsp finely diced green bell pepper
1/2	cup dried bread crumbs
2	pieces pimiento, diced
1/2	cup reduced-fat mayonnaise
1	tsp mustard
1/4	tsp salt
1/4	tsp white pepper
1	lb lump crabmeat, flaked and shell pieces removed

1. Melt the margarine in a small skillet. Sauté the mushrooms and bell pepper for 4 minutes. Remove the vegetables with a slotted spoon and place in a medium bowl.

2. Turn off the heat under the skillet and mix the bread crumbs with the margarine. Set aside. Heat the oven to 350°F.

3. Add the pimiento, mayonnaise, mustard, salt, and pepper to the bowl and mix well. Add the crabmeat, trying to keep large lumps together.

4. Divide the mixture into six ramekins. Sprinkle each ramekin with the bread crumb mixture. Bake for 10 minutes or until lightly brown.

EXCHANGES
1 Starch
2 Lean Meat

Calories 179
Calories from Fat 74
Total Fat . . . . 8 g
Saturated Fat . . . . 1 g
Cholesterol . . . . 53 mg
Sodium . . . . 541 mg
Total Carbohydrate . . . . 11 g
Dietary Fiber . . . . 1 g
Sugars . . . . 2 g
Protein . . . . 15 g

Curtis's Favorite Shrimp

Preparation time: 20 min   Serves 8   Serving size: 1/2 cup

1/2	cup reduced-fat margarine
1	cup sliced fresh mushrooms
1	medium onion, chopped
2	cloves garlic, minced
1	8-oz can chopped tomatoes, with juice
1/4	cup lemon juice
1/4	cup chopped fresh parsley
1/8	tsp salt
	Pepper to taste (optional)
4	Tbsp tomato paste
1 1/2	lb shelled, deveined shrimp
4	cups cooked pasta, any shape

1. Melt the margarine in a large skillet and sauté the mushrooms, onion, and garlic. Add the tomatoes, lemon juice, parsley, salt, and pepper. If the mixture appears thin, add enough tomato paste to thicken.

2. Simmer, uncovered, for 15 minutes. Add the shrimp the last 5 minutes. Spoon over pasta and serve hot.

EXCHANGES
1 Starch
1 Vegetable
2 Lean Meat

Calories 230
   Calories from Fat 56
Total Fat . . . . 6 g
   Saturated Fat . . . . 1 g
Cholesterol . . . . 119 mg
Sodium . . . . 316 mg
Total Carbohydrate . . . . 25 g
   Dietary Fiber . . . . 2 g
   Sugars . . . . 3 g
Protein . . . . 17 g

Daughn's Jerk Fish

Preparation time: 20 min   Serves 4   Serving size: 4 oz

4	whole medium-sized fish (snapper or trout), dressed
1	small onion, finely chopped
6	cloves garlic, finely chopped
2	tsp ground pimiento seeds (available in West Indian markets)
2	Tbsp thyme
1/3–1/2	cup jerk sauce (check the gourmet aisle of your supermarket)
2	Tbsp lite soy sauce
2	tsp olive oil

1. Make two diagonal cuts on either side of each fish. Combine the onion, garlic, ground pimiento seeds, and thyme in a small bowl. Combine the jerk sauce, soy sauce, and olive oil in a shallow dish.

2. Place the seasonings inside the fish. Place the fish in the shallow dish, cover, and marinate overnight or 4–6 hours before baking.

3. Heat the oven to 300°F. Wrap each fish individually in foil and bake for 30 minutes.

EXCHANGES
1/2 Carbohydrate
4 Very Lean Meat

Calories 186
  Calories from Fat 25
Total Fat . . . . 3 g
  Saturated Fat . . . . 0 g
Cholesterol . . . . 52 mg
Sodium . . . . 458 mg
Total Carbohydrate . . . . . 8 g
  Dietary Fiber . . . . 1 g
  Sugars . . . . 6 g
Protein . . . . 30 g

Devona's Crab Cakes

Preparation time: 20 min   Serves 6   Serving size: 1 crab cake

2 cups crabmeat, flaked and shell pieces removed

1 cup dried bread crumbs

1 cup egg substitute

1/2 cup fat-free (skim) evaporated milk

1/2 tsp salt

1/8 tsp dry mustard

1 Tbsp grated onion

1 tsp parsley

1 tsp Worcestershire sauce

1. In a small bowl, mix the crabmeat and bread crumbs together.

2. In a separate bowl, combine the egg substitute and evaporated milk and mix well. Add the crabmeat mixture to the egg and milk mixture.

3. Stir in the salt, mustard, onion, parsley, and Worcestershire sauce. Heat the oven to broil and shape the mixture into six patties. Broil the crab cakes, turning once, until brown, for a total of 7–8 minutes.

EXCHANGES
1 Starch
2 Very Lean Meat

Calories 146
   Calories from Fat 14
Total Fat . . . . 2 g
   Saturated Fat . . . . 0 g
Cholesterol . . . . 34 mg
Sodium . . . . 546 mg
Total Carbohydrate . . . . 17 g
   Dietary Fiber . . . . 0 g
   Sugars . . . . 4 g
Protein . . . . 15 g

Grilled Catfish

Serves 6

6   4-oz catfish fillets
2   Tbsp olive oil
    Juice of 1 lemon
1/2 tsp Dijon mustard
1   Tbsp Worcestershire sauce
1/2 tsp salt
1/2 tsp paprika

1. Heat an outside grill or set the oven to broil. Combine all ingredients except the fish in a small bowl.

2. Place the fish on the grill or broiler and cook for 4–5 minutes on each side, basting frequently with the sauce.

EXCHANGES
3 Lean Meat
1 Fat

Calories 203
  Calories from Fat 106
Total Fat . . . . 12 g
  Saturated Fat . . . . 3 g
Cholesterol . . . . 61 mg
Sodium . . . . 287 mg
Total Carbohydrate . . . . . 1 g
  Dietary Fiber . . . . 0 g
  Sugars . . . . : 1 g
Protein . . . . 21 g

Oven-Fried Fish

Preparation time: 15 min   Serves 8   Serving size: 4 oz

 1   tsp salt

 1   cup nonfat milk

 1   cup dried bread crumbs

 1   tsp basil

 1   tsp oregano

 2   lb dressed fish, cut into bite-sized pieces

 2   Tbsp melted reduced-fat margarine

1. Heat the oven to 500°F. In a shallow dish, mix the salt and milk.

2. In a separate bowl, combine the bread crumbs, basil, and oregano. Dip the fish pieces in the milk and then roll them in the bread crumb mixture.

3. Place the fish in a nonstick baking dish. Pour the melted margarine over the fish and bake 10–12 minutes or until the fish flakes easily with a fork. Serve immediately.

EXCHANGES
1 Starch
3 Very Lean Meat

Calories 186
  Calories from Fat 31
Total Fat . . . . 3 g
  Saturated Fat . . . . 0 g
Cholesterol . . . . 41 mg
Sodium . . . . 494 mg
Total Carbohydrate . . . . 12 g
  Dietary Fiber . . . . 0 g
  Sugars . . . . 2 g
Protein . . . . 26 g

Quick Tuna Casserole

Preparation time: 20 min   Serves 6   Serving size: 1 cup

1	5-oz pkg wide egg noodles
3	cups boiling water
1	10-oz can condensed low-fat mushroom soup
1/3	cup nonfat milk
1	6 1/2-oz can water-packed tuna
1	cup frozen green peas
1	cup dried bread crumbs

1. Cook the noodles in the boiling water about 2 minutes. Cover, remove from heat, and let stand about 10 minutes. Heat the oven to 350°F.

2. Meanwhile, combine the mushroom soup, milk, tuna, and peas in a medium bowl. Rinse the noodles with warm water and drain well. Fold the noodles into the tuna mixture and pour into a nonstick 1-quart casserole.

3. Sprinkle the casserole with bread crumbs and bake for 30 minutes.

EXCHANGES
2 1/2 Starch
1 Very Lean Meat

Calories 248
    Calories from Fat 33
Total Fat . . . . 4 g
    Saturated Fat . . . . 0 g
Cholesterol . . . . 33 mg
Sodium . . . . 681 mg
Total Carbohydrate . . . . 38 g
    Dietary Fiber . . . . 3 g
    Sugars . . . . 4 g
Protein . . . . 16 g

Rogelle's Shrimp Creole

Preparation time: 20 min   Serves 8   Serving size: 1 cup

2	Tbsp corn oil
1 1/2	cups chopped onion
2	tsp minced garlic
	Chopped hot chili pepper (as desired)
1	cup chopped celery
5	medium tomatoes, peeled, seeded, and chopped
	Salt to taste (optional)
	Pepper to taste (optional)
1	Tbsp lime juice
2	bay leaves
1	Tbsp parsley
1	tsp Worcestershire sauce
2	lb peeled and deveined shrimp

1. Heat the oil in a large skillet. Add the onion, garlic, chili pepper, and celery and sauté until the onion is tender. Do not brown.

2. Add the tomatoes, salt, pepper, lime juice, bay leaves, and parsley. Simmer, uncovered, until the sauce is slightly reduced. Remove the bay leaves.

3. Add the Worcestershire sauce and shrimp and cook until the shrimp is done, about 10 minutes. Do not overcook. Serve with hot rice.

EXCHANGES
2 Vegetable
2 Very Lean Meat
1/2 Fat

Calories 152
  Calories from Fat 42
Total Fat . . . . 5 g
  Saturated Fat . . . . 1 g
Cholesterol . . . . 161 mg
Sodium . . . . 215 mg
Total Carbohydrate . . . . . 9 g
  Dietary Fiber . . . . 2 g
  Sugars . . . . 5 g
Protein . . . . 19 g

Salmon Croquette

Preparation time: 15 min   Serves 4   Serving size: 1 patty

1	15 1/2-oz can red salmon, drained
1	medium onion, diced
1/2	medium green bell pepper, diced
1	Tbsp chopped fresh parsley
1/2	Tbsp lemon juice
1/4	cup egg substitute
3	slices whole-wheat bread, crumbled
1/4	tsp pepper
2	Tbsp canola oil

1. In a medium bowl, break the salmon into small pieces with a fork. Remove the bones and skin.

2. Add the onion, bell pepper, parsley, lemon juice, egg substitute, bread, and pepper. Form the mixture into four patties.

3. Heat the oil in a medium skillet and cook the patties over medium heat. Brown for 3 minutes on each side and serve.

EXCHANGES
1 Starch
3 Lean Meat
1/2 Fat

Calories 271
  Calories from Fat 122
Total Fat . . . . 14 g
  Saturated Fat . . . . 0 g
Cholesterol . . . . 52 mg
Sodium . . . . 651 mg
Total Carbohydrate . . . . 15 g
  Dietary Fiber . . . . 2 g
  Sugars . . . . 4 g
Protein . . . . 22 g

Salmon with Lime Sauce

Preparation time: 20 min   Serves 6   Serving size: 3 oz

6   3-oz salmon fillets
1/2   cup flour
1/4   tsp salt
1/2   tsp pepper
2   Tbsp canola oil
1   cup water
2   cups reduced-sodium, fat-free chicken broth
3   Tbsp lime juice
1   Tbsp capers

1. Cut the salmon into six pieces and place them in a plastic bag. Add the flour, salt, and pepper and shake to coat well. Discard the unused flour mixture.

2. Heat the oil in a large skillet. Brown the salmon pieces lightly for 2 minutes on each side.

3. Remove the salmon pieces from the skillet and place them on a plate. Add the water, chicken broth, lime juice, and capers to the skillet and bring the mixture to a boil. Stir well and add the salmon back to the skillet.

4. Reduce the heat and cook the salmon until done, about 5–10 minutes. Serve with a hot baked potato and a salad.

EXCHANGES

1/2 Starch
3 Lean Meat
1/2 Fat

Calories 217
   Calories from Fat 107
Total Fat . . . . 12 g
   Saturated Fat . . . . 1.6 g
Cholesterol . . . . 58 mg
Sodium . . . . 320 mg
Total Carbohydrate . . . . . 6 g
   Dietary Fiber . . . . 0 g
   Sugars . . . . 1 g
Protein . . . . 23 g

Seafood Creole

Preparation time: 20 min   Serves 8   Serving size: 1 cup

1/4	cup corn oil
1/4	cup flour
1	cup hot water
1	lb boneless red snapper, cut into pieces
1	16-oz can tomato sauce
1/2	cup chopped green onion
1/4	cup chopped green bell pepper
4	cloves garlic, minced
1/4	tsp salt
1	tsp thyme
2	bay leaves
1/4	cup chopped fresh parsley
	Dash cayenne pepper

1. Heat the oil in a large skillet and blend in the flour. Stir constantly until flour browns. Be careful not to scorch the roux.

2. Add the water gradually and cook until thick and smooth.

3. Add the remaining ingredients, stir well, and simmer for 15 minutes. Remove the bay leaves before serving over hot rice.

EXCHANGES
1 Vegetable
2 Very Lean Meat
1 1/2 Fat

Calories 153
   Calories from Fat 69
Total Fat . . . . 8 g
   Saturated Fat . . . . 1.1 g
Cholesterol . . . . 21 mg
Sodium . . . . 442 mg
Total Carbohydrate . . . . . 8 g
   Dietary Fiber . . . . 1 g
   Sugars . . . . 4 g
Protein . . . . 13 g

Shrimp and Pasta

Preparation time: 20 min   Serves 10   Serving size: 1 cup

16	oz uncooked linguini noodles
1 1/2	lb cooked, peeled, deveined shrimp
6	oz frozen snow peas, thawed
5	medium tomatoes, chopped
1/3	cup olive oil
1/3	cup wine vinegar
1/4	cup chopped fresh parsley
1	tsp oregano
1/2	tsp garlic powder
1/2	tsp pepper

1. Cook the linguini according to package directions, omitting the salt, and drain. Rinse with cold water and drain again.

2. Place the linguini, shrimp, snow peas, and tomatoes in a large bowl. In a separate bowl, whisk the remaining ingredients together and pour over the pasta. Toss gently to mix. Cover and chill for 2 hours. Serve with warm, crusty bread.

EXCHANGES
2 1/2 Starch
2 Very Lean Meat
1 Fat

Calories 326
    Calories from Fat 81
Total Fat . . . . 9 g
    Saturated Fat . . . . 2 g
Cholesterol . . . . 132 mg
Sodium . . . . 163 mg
Total Carbohydrate . . . . 39 g
    Dietary Fiber . . . . 2 g
    Sugars . . . . 5 g
Protein . . . . 21 g

Shrimp and Rice

Preparation time: 20 min   Serves 8   Serving size: 1/2 cup

1	Tbsp canola oil
1	medium onion, chopped
1	medium green bell pepper, chopped
1 1/2	lb cooked, peeled shrimp, chopped
8	oz tomato sauce
4	cups water
1/2	tsp thyme
2	bay leaves
1/2	tsp salt
1/2	tsp garlic powder
2	cups uncooked rice

1. Heat the oil in a large saucepan and sauté the onion and bell pepper until slightly tender. Add the shrimp, tomato sauce, water, thyme, bay leaves, and seasonings. Simmer 3 minutes.

2. Add the rice, stir well, and simmer on low heat for 20 minutes.

EXCHANGES
2 1/2 Starch
1 Vegetable
2 Very Lean Meat

Calories 290
  Calories from Fat 28
Total Fat . . . . 3 g
  Saturated Fat . . . . 0 g
Cholesterol . . . . 165 mg
Sodium . . . . 522 mg
Total Carbohydrate . . . . 42 g
  Dietary Fiber . . . . 1 g
  Sugars . . . . 3 g
Protein . . . . 22 g

Shrimp Fried Rice

Preparation time: 20 min   Serves 8   Serving size: 1 cup

2	tsp sesame oil
1	cup chopped green onion
1/2	cup chopped green bell pepper
1/2	cup chopped celery
1	cup sliced mushrooms
1 1/2	lb peeled and deveined shrimp
3	cups cooked rice
1/2	cup bean sprouts
1/8	tsp salt
1	tsp pepper
1	tsp garlic powder
2	Tbsp lite soy sauce
1	cup egg substitute

1. Heat the oil in a large wok or skillet. Stir-fry the onion, bell pepper, celery, and mushrooms for 5 minutes. Add the shrimp and stir-fry until pink.

2. Add the rice, bean sprouts, salt, pepper, garlic powder, and soy sauce. Stir-fry for 10 minutes.

3. Make a hole in the middle of the mixture and pour in the egg substitute. Cook the egg until done and mix into rice mixture. Serve hot.

EXCHANGES
1 1/2 Starch
2 Very Lean Meat

Calories 206
  Calories from Fat 21
Total Fat . . . . 2 g
  Saturated Fat . . . . 0 g
Cholesterol . . . . 129 mg
Sodium . . . . 379 mg
Total Carbohydrate . . . . 22 g
  Dietary Fiber . . . . 1 g
  Sugars . . . . 3 g
Protein . . . . 23 g

Shrimp Jambalaya

Preparation time: 20 min   Serves 8   Serving size: 3/4 cup

      2   Tbsp olive oil
  1 1/2   lb peeled and deveined shrimp
      1   medium onion, chopped
      1   medium green bell pepper, chopped
      2   cups cooked rice
      1   16-oz can tomato sauce
      1   tsp Cajun seasoning
           Salt to taste (optional)
           Pepper to taste (optional)
           Hot pepper sauce to taste (optional)

1. Heat the oil in a large skillet and sauté the shrimp, onion, and bell pepper until the shrimp is pink.

2. Stir in the remaining ingredients and cook until heated through.

EXCHANGES
1 Starch
1 Vegetable
2 Very Lean Meat
1/2 Fat

Calories 203
   Calories from Fat 32
Total Fat . . . . 4 g
   Saturated Fat . . . . 1 g
Cholesterol . . . . 129 mg
Sodium . . . . 626 mg
Total Carbohydrate . . . . 19 g
   Dietary Fiber . . . . 1 g
   Sugars . . . . 5 g
Protein . . . . 20 g

Spicy Shrimp

Preparation time: 20 min   Serves 6   Serving size: 1/2 cup

1 1/2	lb uncooked, peeled, and deveined shrimp
1	Tbsp rum
1/4	cup vinegar
2	Tbsp lite soy sauce
4	tsp sugar
2	tsp cornstarch
2	Tbsp sesame oil
3	cloves garlic, minced
1/4	tsp red pepper flakes
1/2	cup bamboo shoots
2	stalks green onion, thinly sliced
1 1/2	Tbsp minced fresh ginger
2	stalks celery, cut into 1/2-inch slices

1. In a medium bowl, toss the shrimp with the rum. In a separate bowl, combine the vinegar, soy sauce, sugar, and cornstarch.

2. Heat the oil in a large wok or skillet and stir-fry the garlic, red pepper flakes, bamboo shoots, onion, ginger, and celery for 3 minutes.

3. Add the shrimp and stir-fry until the shrimp just turns pink. Add the sauce and cook until the sauce bubbles and thickens. Serve with steamed rice.

EXCHANGES
1 Vegetable
2 Lean Meat

Calories 143
Calories from Fat 49
Total Fat . . . . 5 g
Saturated Fat . . . . 1 g
Cholesterol . . . . 160 mg
Sodium . . . . 398 mg
Total Carbohydrate . . . . . 4 g
Dietary Fiber . . . . 1 g
Sugars . . . . 3 g
Protein . . . . 18 g

Key Lime Pie

Chicken Fricassee with Rice
Southern Spiced Tea

Salmon Croquette

Spicy Shrimp

Vegetables and Sides

Baked Acorn Squash

1	medium acorn squash
2	tsp honey
1/4	tsp nutmeg
1/4	tsp cinnamon
1/4	tsp cloves
1	Tbsp reduced-fat margarine

1. Heat the oven to 350°F. Cut the squash lengthwise and remove the seeds and fibers. Place the squash in a baking dish and cover with 1/2 inch of water.

2. Sprinkle with honey and spices and dot with margarine. Bake, covered, for 30 minutes. Uncover for the last 10 minutes of cooking to brown. The squash should be tender when touched with a fork.

EXCHANGES
1/2 Starch
1/2 Fat

Calories 51
   Calories from Fat 17
Total Fat . . . . 2 g
   Saturated Fat . . . . 0 g
Cholesterol . . . . 0 mg
Sodium . . . . 25 mg
Total Carbohydrate . . . . . 9 g
   Dietary Fiber . . . . 2 g
   Sugars . . . . 5 g
Protein . . . . 1 g

Boiled Rutabagas

Preparation time: 15 min   Serves 6   Serving size: 1/2 cup

2   large rutabagas
1   medium onion, chopped
3   oz smoked turkey breast

1. Peel the rutabagas and chop into cubes. Place the rutabagas in a large saucepan and add the onion and turkey. Fill the pan halfway with water.

2. Bring to a boil and then reduce heat. Cover and simmer until the rutabagas are tender, about 30–45 minutes.

EXCHANGES
1 Starch

Calories 88
   Calories from Fat 5
Total Fat . . . . 1 g
   Saturated Fat . . . . 0 g
Cholesterol . . . . 7 mg
Sodium . . . . 205 mg
Total Carbohydrate . . . . 17 g
   Dietary Fiber . . . . 3 g
   Sugars . . . . 11 g
Protein . . . . 5 g

Broccoli Casserole

Preparation time: 15 min   Serves 12   Serving size: 1/2 cup

Nonstick cooking spray
2   12-oz pkgs frozen chopped broccoli, defrosted
1/2   cup egg substitute
1   10-oz can 98% fat-free cream of celery soup
1   medium onion, finely chopped
1   tsp chopped garlic
1/4   tsp pepper
2   tsp reduced-fat margarine
1 1/2   cups stuffing mix
2   oz shredded reduced-fat cheddar cheese

1. Heat the oven to 350°F. Spray a 13 × 9 × 12-inch baking dish with nonstick cooking spray and place the broccoli in the dish. Mix the egg, soup, onion, garlic, and pepper together and pour over the broccoli.

2. Melt the margarine and stir it into the stuffing mix. Pour the stuffing over the broccoli and spread evenly.
Bake for 30 minutes. Sprinkle cheese on top and return to oven for 5 minutes or until cheese melts. Let stand 10 minutes before serving.

EXCHANGES
1/2 Starch
1 Vegetable
1/2 Fat

Calories 81
  Calories from Fat 19
Total Fat . . . . 2 g
  Saturated Fat . . . . 0.8 g
Cholesterol . . . . 4 mg
Sodium . . . . 339 mg
Total Carbohydrate . . . . 11 g
  Dietary Fiber . . . . 2 g
  Sugars . . . . 2 g
Protein . . . . 5 g

Butter Beans with Smoked Turkey

Preparation time: 10 min   Serves 8   Serving size: 1 cup

8	oz smoked turkey breast
1/4	cup chopped onion
1	lb dried butter beans (mature lima beans), soaked overnight
1	clove garlic, minced
1/8	tsp pepper
1	bay leaf
1	tsp thyme
1/4	tsp salt

1. Boil the turkey and onion in 1 quart of water for 45 minutes.

2. Place the beans, garlic, pepper, bay leaf, and thyme in the water and cook for 1 hour or until the beans are tender. Add the salt in the final 15 minutes of cooking to prevent the beans from becoming tough.

EXCHANGES
2 1/2 Starch
1 Very Lean Meat

Calories 216
  Calories from Fat 6
Total Fat . . . . 1 g
  Saturated Fat . . . . 0 g
Cholesterol . . . . 13 mg
Sodium . . . . 423 mg
Total Carbohydrate . . . . 36 g
  Dietary Fiber . . . . 11 g
  Sugars . . . . 5 g
Protein . . . . 18 g

Cabbage Casserole

Preparation time: 20 min Serves 8 Serving size: 1 cup

1 lb 96% extra-lean ground beef
1 medium onion, chopped
1/2 cup uncooked rice
1 medium head green cabbage, shredded
8 oz tomato sauce
1/2 tsp salt
1 cup water

1. Heat the oven to 350°F. In a medium skillet, brown the ground beef and onion. Drain the beef mixture and transfer it to a large baking dish.

2. Sprinkle the rice over the mixture. Spread the shredded cabbage evenly over the beef. Add the tomato sauce, salt, and water. Bake, tightly covered, for 50–60 minutes or until the rice is tender.

EXCHANGES
1/2 Starch
2 Vegetable
1 Lean Meat

Calories 164
Calories from Fat 29
Total Fat . . . . 3 g
Saturated Fat . . . . 1.4 g
Cholesterol . . . . 34 mg
Sodium . . . . 374 mg
Total Carbohydrate . . . . 20 g
Dietary Fiber . . . . 4 g
Sugars . . . . 7 g
Protein . . . . 14 g

Collard Greens

Preparation time: 20 min   Serves 8   Serving size: 1 cup

4 lb collard greens

3 cups reduced-sodium, reduced-fat chicken broth

2 medium onions, chopped

3 whole garlic cloves, crushed

1 tsp red pepper flakes

1 tsp pepper

1. Wash and cut the collard greens and place them in a large stockpot. Add the remaining ingredients and enough water to cover.

2. Cook until tender, stirring occasionally, about 3 1/2 hours. The flavors will blend even more if you let the greens sit for a bit after cooking.

EXCHANGES

3 Vegetable

Calories 78
   Calories from Fat 4
Total Fat . . . . 0 g
   Saturated Fat . . . . 0 g
Cholesterol . . . . 0 mg
Sodium . . . . 240 mg
Total Carbohydrate . . . . 16 g
   Dietary Fiber . . . . 6 g
   Sugars . . . . 3 g
Protein . . . . 4 g

Collards with Smoked Turkey

Preparation time: 20 min   Serves 8   Serving size: 1 cup

4	lb collard greens
1/4	lb smoked turkey breast
3	cups reduced-sodium, reduced-fat chicken broth
2	medium onions, chopped
3	whole garlic cloves, crushed
1	tsp red pepper flakes
1	tsp pepper

1. Wash and cut the collard greens and place them in a large stockpot. Add the remaining ingredients and enough water to cover.

2. Cook until tender, stirring occasionally, about 3 1/2 hours. The flavors will blend even more if you let the greens sit for a bit after cooking.

EXCHANGES
3 Vegetable

Calories	91
Calories from Fat	6
Total Fat	1 g
Saturated Fat	0 g
Cholesterol	7 mg
Sodium	410 mg
Total Carbohydrate	16 g
Dietary Fiber	6 g
Sugars	3 g
Protein	7 g

Creamed Potatoes

1   lb potatoes, washed, peeled, and cut into quarters
1   cup fat-free (skim) evaporated milk
2   tsp reduced-fat margarine
2   Tbsp chives
1   tsp salt
1   tsp white pepper
3   Tbsp water

1. Boil the potatoes for 20–30 minutes or until done.

2. Drain the potatoes and add the remaining ingredients. Whip well.

EXCHANGES
1 Starch

Calories 91
  Calories from Fat 7
Total Fat . . . . 1 g
  Saturated Fat . . . . 0 g
Cholesterol . . . . 2 mg
Sodium . . . . 450 mg
Total Carbohydrate . . . . 17 g
  Dietary Fiber . . . . 1 g
  Sugars . . . . 5 g
Protein . . . . 4 g

Field Peas

Preparation time: 10 min   Serves 6   Serving size: 1 cup

2	cups water
8	oz fresh chicken or turkey necks
1	medium onion, chopped
1	clove garlic, minced
1	tsp parsley
1	lb fresh or frozen field peas
1/2	tsp salt
1/4	tsp red pepper flakes
	Pepper to taste (optional)

1. In a large stockpot, boil the water. Add the chicken or turkey necks, onion, garlic, and parsley and boil for 15 minutes.

2. Add the field peas and cook until tender, about 30 minutes. Add the salt, pepper flakes, and pepper. Serve over steamed rice.

EXCHANGES
1 1/2 Starch
1 Very Lean Meat

Calories 148
   Calories from Fat 16
Total Fat . . . . 2 g
   Saturated Fat . . . . 1 g
Cholesterol . . . . 23 mg
Sodium . . . . 207 mg
Total Carbohydrate . . . . 22 g
   Dietary Fiber . . . . 7 g
   Sugars . . . . 3 g
Protein . . . . 12 g

Fried Green Tomatoes

> 4   firm green tomatoes
> 1   cup cornmeal
>   Salt to taste (optional)
>   Pepper to taste (optional)
> 3   Tbsp canola oil

1. Wash the tomatoes, remove the stems, and slice each tomato into four thick slices. Season the cornmeal with salt and pepper.

2. Heat the oil in a medium skillet until hot. Dip the tomato slices into the cornmeal and fry until brown, turning once, about 3–4 minutes total.

EXCHANGES
2 Starch
2 Fat

Calories	251
Calories from Fat	102
Total Fat	11 g
Saturated Fat	0 g
Cholesterol	0 mg
Sodium	17 mg
Total Carbohydrate	33 g
Dietary Fiber	4 g
Sugars	3 g
Protein	4 g

Fried Okra

1	lb fresh okra
1	cup egg substitute
1/8	tsp salt
2	Tbsp water
1	cup yellow cornmeal
1/4	cup canola oil
	Salt to taste (optional)
	Pepper to taste (optional)

1. Wash the okra, trim the ends, and cut each piece in half. Beat egg substitute, salt, and water. Dip the okra into the egg mixture and roll in the cornmeal to coat.

2. Heat the oil in a medium skillet until hot. Fry the okra until brown, about 10–15 minutes. Season with salt and pepper to taste.

EXCHANGES
1 1/2 Starch
1 Vegetable
2 Fat

Calories	244
Calories from Fat	117
Total Fat	13 g
Saturated Fat	0 g
Cholesterol	0 mg
Sodium	126 mg
Total Carbohydrate	24 g
Dietary Fiber	3 g
Sugars	2 g
Protein	8 g

Garlic Mashed Potatoes

Preparation time: 10 min   Serves 6   Serving size: 1/2 cup

4   medium potatoes, peeled and cubed
7   cloves garlic, minced
1/3   cup nonfat milk, heated
1/4   cup fat-free sour cream
2   Tbsp reduced-fat margarine
      Salt to taste (optional)
      Pepper to taste (optional)

1. Boil the potatoes over medium heat until tender and drain them.

2. Add the garlic and mash the potatoes. Add the milk, sour cream, margarine, salt, and pepper and mix well until smooth.

EXCHANGES
1 Starch
1/2 Fat

Calories 99
    Calories from Fat 18
Total Fat . . . . 2 g
    Saturated Fat . . . . 0 g
Cholesterol . . . . 0 mg
Sodium . . . . 61 mg
Total Carbohydrate . . . . 18 g
    Dietary Fiber . . . . 1 g
    Sugars . . . . 4 g
Protein . . . . 3 g

Green Beans and New Potatoes

Preparation time: 10 min Serves 6 Serving size: 1 cup

2   16-oz bags frozen green beans
8   new potatoes, washed, peeled, and halved
1   medium onion, chopped
4   oz smoked turkey breast

1. Add all ingredients to a large stockpot and cover with water. Bring to a boil, and then reduce heat.

2. Cook until the green beans and new potatoes are tender, about 20 minutes.

EXCHANGES
1 Starch
2 Vegetable

Calories 117
    Calories from Fat 5
Total Fat . . . . 1 g
    Saturated Fat . . . . 0 g
Cholesterol . . . . 9 mg
Sodium . . . . 242 mg
Total Carbohydrate . . . . 23 g
    Dietary Fiber . . . . 5 g
    Sugars . . . . 6 g
Protein . . . . 7 g

Luscious Lima Beans

Preparation time: 10 min   Serves 8   Serving size: 1/2 cup

4   oz smoked turkey breast
2   8-oz bags frozen lima beans
1   medium onion, chopped
1   clove garlic, minced

1. Put the turkey into a medium pot and cover with water. Boil for 30 minutes.

2. Add the remaining ingredients and cook until the lima beans are tender, about 20 minutes. Serve with corn bread (see recipe on p. 112).

EXCHANGES
1 Starch

Calories 83
   Calories from Fat 4
Total Fat . . . . 0 g
   Saturated Fat . . . . 0 g
Cholesterol . . . . 7 mg
Sodium . . . . 204 mg
Total Carbohydrate . . . . 14 g
   Dietary Fiber . . . . 4 g
   Sugars . . . . 3 g
Protein . . . . 7 g

Orange Carrots

- 2   lb baby carrots
- 2   Tbsp brown sugar
- 2   Tbsp reduced-fat margarine
- 1/4   cup orange juice concentrate, thawed
- 1/2   cup mandarin orange pieces
- 1/4   tsp salt
- 1   medium Vidalia onion, thinly sliced

1. Heat the oven to 350°F. Boil the carrots until tender and drain them.

2. In a separate bowl, combine the remaining ingredients and mix well. Place the carrots in a baking dish and cover with the sauce.

3. Stir once to coat the carrots. Bake for 15–20 minutes.

EXCHANGES
1/2 Fruit
3 Vegetable

Calories	101
Calories from Fat	13
Total Fat	1 g
Saturated Fat	0.1 g
Cholesterol	0 mg
Sodium	177 mg
Total Carbohydrate	22 g
Dietary Fiber	4 g
Sugars	14 g
Protein	2 g

Orange Sweet Potatoes

Preparation time: 20 min   Serves 8   Serving size: 1/2 cup

5 medium oranges, unpeeled
1/3 cup brown sugar
1/2 cup brandy
1/4 cup fat-free (skim) evaporated milk
2 Tbsp reduced-fat margarine
1/2 tsp salt
4 cups cooked, mashed sweet potatoes
Dash nutmeg

1. Grate the peel from one orange. Cut the remaining oranges in half. Scoop out the pulp to yield 2 cups of drained fruit and save the shells.

2. Cut a thin slice from the bottom of each orange shell to make it sit flat. Sprinkle the orange pulp with brown sugar and set aside.

3. Heat the oven to 350°F. In a medium saucepan, heat the brandy, evaporated milk, margarine, and salt. Add to the sweet potatoes and mix well.

4. Stuff each of the eight orange shells with 1/2 cup of the sweet potato mixture. Sprinkle each shell with grated orange peel. Bake for 30 minutes. Garnish with a dash of nutmeg.

EXCHANGES
2 1/2 Carbohydrate

Calories 189
  Calories from Fat 14
Total Fat . . . . 2 g
  Saturated Fat . . . . 0 g
Cholesterol . . . . 0 mg
Sodium . . . . 191 mg
Total Carbohydrate . . . . 40 g
  Dietary Fiber . . . . 4 g
  Sugars . . . . 25 g
Protein . . . . 3 g

Rutabaga Soufflé

Preparation time: 15 min   Serves 8   Serving size: 1/2 cup

1   large rutabaga
1   tsp sugar
1   cup fat-free sour cream
2   Tbsp reduced-fat margarine
1   tsp baking powder
    Salt to taste (optional)
    Pepper to taste (optional)
4   egg whites
1/2   cup dried bread crumbs
    Dash nutmeg

1. Peel the rutabaga and boil in a saucepan with the sugar and enough water to cover for 20–30 minutes. Drain and mash the rutabaga to yield 2 cups.

2. Heat the oven to 350°F. In a medium bowl, combine the rutabaga, sour cream, margarine, baking powder, salt, pepper, and two egg whites.

3. In a separate bowl, beat the remaining two egg whites until stiff. Fold the egg whites into the rutabaga mixture. Pour into 1 1/2-quart casserole dish. Sprinkle with the bread crumbs and nutmeg.

4. Bake for 30 minutes.

EXCHANGES
1 Carbohydrate

Calories 96
  Calories from Fat 15
Total Fat . . . . 2 g
  Saturated Fat . . . . 0.2 g
Cholesterol . . . . 2 mg
Sodium . . . . 192 mg
Total Carbohydrate . . . . 16 g
  Dietary Fiber . . . . 1 g
  Sugars . . . . 6 g
Protein . . . . 4 g

Smothered Cabbage

Preparation time: 20 min   Serves 6   Serving size: 1 cup

1	medium head green cabbage
1	Tbsp canola oil
1	medium green bell pepper, seeded and chopped
1	tsp caraway seeds
1/8	tsp salt
	Pepper to taste (optional)

1. Wash and quarter the cabbage and pat dry. Heat the oil in a large skillet. Add the bell pepper and sauté until limp, about 5 minutes.

2. Add the cabbage, caraway seeds, salt, and pepper. Cover tightly and cook over medium heat until the cabbage is just tender (cabbage becomes mushy when overcooked), about 15–20 minutes.

EXCHANGES
1 Vegetable
1/2 Fat

Calories 60
   Calories from Fat 27
Total Fat . . . . 3 g
   Saturated Fat . . . . 0 g
Cholesterol . . . . 0 mg
Sodium . . . . 58 mg
Total Carbohydrate . . . . 8 g
   Dietary Fiber . . . . 4 g
   Sugars . . . . 3 g
Protein . . . . 2 g

Steamed Cabbage

Preparation time: 10 min   Serves 6   Serving size: 1 cup

1	Tbsp olive oil
3	oz smoked turkey, cut into pieces
1/3	cup water
1	medium head cabbage, chopped
1/8	tsp salt
1/8	tsp pepper

1. Heat the oil in a large saucepan and sauté the turkey for 5 minutes.

2. Add the remaining ingredients and cook the cabbage just until tender (cabbage becomes mushy when overcooked), about 15–20 minutes.

EXCHANGES
1 Vegetable
1/2 Fat

Calories 65
   Calories from Fat 27
Total Fat . . . . 3 g
   Saturated Fat . . . . 1 g
Cholesterol . . . . 7 mg
Sodium . . . . 228 mg
Total Carbohydrate . . . . . 6 g
   Dietary Fiber . . . . 3 g
   Sugars . . . . 2 g
Protein . . . . 4 g

Stewed Tomatoes and Okra

Preparation time: 15 min   Serves 8   Serving size: 1 cup

8	large fresh tomatoes
2	tsp reduced-fat margarine
2	medium onions, chopped
1	green bell pepper, seeded and chopped
16	oz frozen or fresh okra
1	cup frozen corn
2	tsp sugar
1/2	cup dried bread crumbs

1. Plunge tomatoes in boiling water for 1 minute to make them easier to peel. Peel and chop the tomatoes.

2. Heat the margarine in a large skillet and sauté the tomatoes, onions, and bell pepper. Add the okra, corn, and sugar and simmer for 25 minutes. To thicken, add the bread crumbs and stir well.

EXCHANGES
1 Starch
2 Vegetable

Calories	128
Calories from Fat	20
Total Fat	2 g
Saturated Fat	0 g
Cholesterol	0 mg
Sodium	85 mg
Total Carbohydrate	26 g
Dietary Fiber	5 g
Sugars	10 g
Protein	5 g

Sweet Potato Soufflé

Preparation time: 25 min   Serves 6   Serving size: 1/2 cup

4	lb sweet potatoes
2	Tbsp sugar
1/2	cup brown sugar
1/4	cup raisins
1	tsp nutmeg
1/2	cup fat-free (skim) evaporated milk
1/3	cup reduced-fat margarine
1	cup egg substitute
1/4	cup chopped pecans
1/2	tsp salt
	Juice of 1 lemon
	Nonstick cooking spray
1/2	cup miniature marshmallows

1. Peel and boil the sweet potatoes. Heat the oven to 350°F.

2. Drain and mash the sweet potatoes. Place them in a large bowl and add all ingredients, except marshmallows. Stir well.

3. Spray a casserole dish with nonstick cooking spray. Place the sweet potatoes in the casserole dish and bake for 30 minutes.

4. Change the oven setting to broil, sprinkle the marshmallows over the sweet potatoes, and place under broiler until the marshmallows melt.

EXCHANGES
3 Carbohydrate
1/2 Fat

Calories 238
   Calories from Fat 38
Total Fat . . . . 4 g
   Saturated Fat . . . . 0 g
Cholesterol . . . . 0 mg
Sodium . . . . 203 mg
Total Carbohydrate . . . . 46 g
   Dietary Fiber . . . . 4 g
   Sugars . . . . 29 g
Protein . . . . 5 g

Turnip Greens with Bottoms

Preparation time: 20 min   Serves 8   Serving size: 1 cup

2   large bunches turnip greens with turnips
8   oz smoked turkey breast
1   large onion, chopped
    Red pepper flakes

1. Wash the turnip greens thoroughly and cut into pieces. Peel the turnips and chop into small pieces.

2. Boil the turkey in water until the turkey is tender, about 20 minutes. Add the turnip greens, turnips, onion, and red pepper flakes and cook until done, about 20 minutes.

EXCHANGES
1 Vegetable
1 Very Lean Meat

Calories 59
   Calories from Fat 5
Total Fat . . . . 1 g
   Saturated Fat . . . . 0 g
Cholesterol . . . . 13 mg
Sodium . . . . 394 mg
Total Carbohydrate . . . . . 8 g
   Dietary Fiber . . . . 4 g
   Sugars . . . . 4 g
Protein . . . . 7 g

Breads, Cereals, and Grains

Baked Cheese Grits

Preparation time: 20 min   Serves 9   Serving size: 1/2 cup

4	cups water
1/2	tsp salt
1	cup grits
3	Tbsp flour
3/4	cup shredded reduced-fat sharp cheddar cheese
1/4	cup chopped green onion
1	tsp minced garlic
1/2	cup egg substitute

1. Boil the water and add the salt and grits. Cook, covered, over low heat for 20 minutes. Meanwhile, heat the oven to 350°F.

2. Stir the flour, cheese, green onion, garlic, and egg substitute into the grits. Pour into a nonstick 8 × 8 × 2-inch baking pan and bake for 30 minutes, until a knife inserted near the center comes out clean.

EXCHANGES
1 Starch
1/2 Fat

Calories 110
    Calories from Fat 20
Total Fat . . . . 2 g
    Saturated Fat . . . . 1.2 g
Cholesterol . . . . 7 mg
Sodium . . . . 236 mg
Total Carbohydrate . . . . 17 g
    Dietary Fiber . . . . 0 g
    Sugars . . . . 1 g
Protein . . . . 6 g

Banana Bread

Preparation time: 20 min   Serves 10   Serving size: 1 slice

Nonstick cooking spray
1 1/2   cups flour
1 1/2   tsp baking powder
1/4   tsp baking soda
1/4   tsp cinnamon
1/4   tsp nutmeg
1/8   tsp salt
1   egg
3   medium soft bananas, mashed
3/4   cup sugar
1/4   cup canola oil
1   tsp finely shredded lemon peel
1/4   cup coconut flakes

1. Spray a 2 × 4 × 2-inch loaf pan with nonstick cooking spray and heat the oven to 350°F. In a medium mixing bowl, combine the flour, baking powder, baking soda, cinnamon, nutmeg, and salt. Make a well in the center of the dry mixture and set aside.

2. In a blender or food processor, combine the egg, bananas, sugar, oil, lemon peel, and coconut. Add the egg mixture all at once to the dry mixture. Stir just until moistened (do not overbeat).

3. Spoon the batter into the prepared pan. Bake for 50–55 minutes or until a wooden toothpick inserted near the center comes out clean. Remove from the pan and cool on a wire rack.

EXCHANGES
2 1/2 Carbohydrate
1 Fat

Calories 227
　Calories from Fat 63
Total Fat . . . . 7 g
　Saturated Fat . . . . 1 g
Cholesterol . . . . 21 mg
Sodium . . . . 126 mg
Total Carbohydrate . . . . 39 g
　Dietary Fiber . . . . 1 g
　Sugars . . . . 22 g
Protein . . . . 3 g

Charlie's Corn Casserole

Preparation time: 15 min   Serves 8   Serving size: 1/2 cup

1   8-oz can creamed corn
1   cup canned whole kernel corn, undrained
2   tsp sugar
1   cup egg substitute
1   6 1/2-oz pkg corn bread mix
1   Tbsp corn oil

1. Heat the oven to 350°F. In a large bowl, mix all the ingredients together, including the liquid from the corn.

2. Pour the batter into a nonstick loaf pan and bake for 45 minutes or until puffed and golden.

EXCHANGES
2 Starch

Calories 156
   Calories from Fat 25
Total Fat . . . . 3 g
   Saturated Fat . . . . 1 g
Cholesterol . . . . 0 mg
Sodium . . . . 337 mg
Total Carbohydrate . . . . 29 g
   Dietary Fiber . . . . 2 g
   Sugars . . . . 9 g
Protein . . . . 6 g

Corn Bread

Preparation time: 15 min　　　Serves 8　　　Serving size: 1 piece

　　1　cup yellow cornmeal
　1/2　cup flour
　　2　tsp baking powder
　1/2　tsp salt
1 1/2　cups nonfat milk
　　1　cup egg substitute
　　1　Tbsp canola oil

1. Heat the oven to 425°F. In a large bowl, mix the dry ingredients together. Add the milk, egg substitute, and oil to the dry ingredients and mix well.

2. Pour the batter into a 13 × 9-inch nonstick loaf pan and bake for 30 minutes.

EXCHANGES
1 1/2 Starch

Calories 142
　Calories from Fat 20
Total Fat . . . . 2 g
　Saturated Fat . . . . 0 g
Cholesterol . . . . 1 mg
Sodium . . . . 315 mg
Total Carbohydrate . . . . 23 g
　Dietary Fiber . . . . 1 g
　Sugars . . . . 3 g
Protein . . . . 7 g

Corn Bread Casserole

Preparation time: 15 min   Serves 6   Serving size: 1/2 cup

1	cup yellow cornmeal
1/2	tsp baking soda
1/4	tsp salt
8	oz plain fat-free yogurt
1	8-oz can creamed corn
1/4	cup fat-free (skim) evaporated milk

1. Heat the oven to 350°F. In a large bowl, combine the dry ingredients. Add the remaining ingredients and stir just until moistened (do not overbeat).

2. Pour the batter into six individual soufflé cups and bake for 30 minutes or until a knife inserted in the cups comes out clean. Serve hot.

EXCHANGES
2 Starch

Calories 138
   Calories from Fat 5
Total Fat . . . . 1 g
   Saturated Fat . . . . 0 g
Cholesterol . . . . 1 mg
Sodium . . . . 351 mg
Total Carbohydrate . . . . 29 g
   Dietary Fiber . . . . 2 g
   Sugars . . . . 7 g
Protein . . . . 5 g

Corn Bread Dressing

Preparation time: 25 min   Serves 10   Serving size: 1/2 cup

3	Tbsp reduced-fat margarine
1	cup chopped onion
2	cups chopped celery
2	cloves garlic, crushed
1/4	cup parsley
6	slices whole-wheat bread, dried
5	cups leftover corn bread (see recipe, p. 112)
1	tsp thyme
2	tsp sage
1	tsp marjoram
1	tsp pepper
1/2	tsp salt
2	cups egg substitute
2	cups turkey broth (from boiling giblets without salt, or use canned)

1. Heat the margarine in a large skillet and sauté the onion, celery, garlic, and parsley for 10 minutes. Put the whole-wheat bread and corn bread in a large bowl and crumble up into small pieces.

2. Heat the oven to 350°F. Add the spices to the bread and mix well. Add the onion mixture and stir.

3. Add the egg substitute and mix well; then add cool turkey broth and stir. Pour the dressing into a nonstick baking pan and bake for 45 minutes. For variety, try adding chestnuts, mushrooms, olives, or reduced-fat sausage to this dressing.

EXCHANGES
2 Starch
1 Fat

Calories 212
    Calories from Fat 38
Total Fat . . . . 4 g
    Saturated Fat . . . . 0 g
Cholesterol . . . . 1 mg
Sodium . . . . 585 mg
Total Carbohydrate . . . . 30 g
    Dietary Fiber . . . . 3 g
    Sugars . . . . 5 g
Protein . . . . 13 g

Corn Muffins

Preparation time: 15 min   Serves 12   Serving size: 1 muffin

1	cup boiling water
1	cup yellow cornmeal
1/2	tsp salt
2	tsp baking powder
2	tsp reduced-fat margarine
1/2	cup nonfat milk
1/2	cup egg substitute
2	tsp sugar

1. In a large bowl, pour the boiling water over the cornmeal and stir well. Allow to cool.

2. Heat the oven to 425°F. Add all ingredients to the bowl, mix, pour the batter into nonstick muffin pans, and bake for 25 minutes or until light brown.

EXCHANGES
1/2 Starch

Calories 57
Calories from Fat 5
Total Fat . . . . 1 g
Saturated Fat . . . . 0 g
Cholesterol . . . . 0 mg
Sodium . . . . 186 mg
Total Carbohydrate . . . . 11 g
Dietary Fiber . . . . 1 g
Sugars . . . . 1 g
Protein . . . . 2 g

Corn Pudding

Preparation time: 20 min   Serves 8   Serving size: 1/2 cup

2	cups grated fresh corn kernels (about 12 ears)
1	Tbsp flour
1	Tbsp sugar
1	tsp salt
1/4	tsp pepper
1	Tbsp reduced-fat margarine
1	cup egg substitute
1	cup fat-free (skim) evaporated milk

1. Grate the corn from the ears into a large bowl. Add the flour, sugar, salt, and pepper to the corn and stir.

2. Heat the oven to 325°F. Melt the margarine in a separate dish. In a separate bowl, beat the egg substitute, margarine, and milk for 3 minutes and add to the corn mixture.

3. Pour the pudding into a nonstick loaf pan and place in the oven in a hot water bath. Bake for 30 minutes or until the pudding is firm to the touch.

EXCHANGES
1 Starch

Calories 103
   Calories from Fat 12
Total Fat . . . . 1 g
   Saturated Fat . . . . 0 g
Cholesterol . . . . 1 mg
Sodium . . . . 401 mg
Total Carbohydrate . . . . 17 g
   Dietary Fiber . . . . 1 g
   Sugars . . . . 6 g
Protein . . . . 7 g

Dill Drop Biscuits

Preparation time: 15 min   Serves 8   Serving size: 1 biscuit

1	cup unbleached flour
2	tsp baking powder
1/4	tsp salt
1	tsp dill
1/2	cup low-fat buttermilk
1/4	cup canola oil

1. Heat the oven to 425°F. Place the dry ingredients in a medium bowl. Add the buttermilk and oil and stir just enough to moisten the dry ingredients.

2. Drop tablespoonfuls of batter onto a nonstick baking sheet and bake for 15 minutes. Serve hot.

EXCHANGES
1 Starch
1 Fat

Calories 128
   Calories from Fat 66
Total Fat . . . . 7 g
   Saturated Fat . . . . 0 g
Cholesterol . . . . 1 mg
Sodium . . . . 180 mg
Total Carbohydrate . . . . 13 g
   Dietary Fiber . . . . 0 g
   Sugars . . . . 1 g
Protein . . . . 2 g

Doc's French Toast

2   cups egg substitute

2   Tbsp sugar

1/2   tsp cinnamon

1/2   tsp nutmeg

1   tsp vanilla extract

8   slices white bread

1. Mix the batter ingredients together in a medium bowl and stir well. Dip the bread slices into the batter and turn quickly to coat both sides evenly.

2. Place on a hot nonstick griddle and brown. Serve with reduced-calorie syrup or fresh fruit.

EXCHANGES
1 Starch
1 Very Lean Meat

Calories 101
   Calories from Fat 8
Total Fat . . . . 1 g
   Saturated Fat . . . . 0 g
Cholesterol . . . . 0 mg
Sodium . . . . 218 mg
Total Carbohydrate . . . . 15 g
   Dietary Fiber . . . . 1 g
   Sugars . . . . 5 g
Protein . . . . 8 g

Ernestine's Pigeon Peas and Rice

Preparation time: 20 min   Serves 8   Serving size: 1 cup

1	Tbsp canola oil
1	medium onion, chopped
1	medium green bell pepper, seeded and chopped
1	can pigeon peas (check the Hispanic food aisle in your supermarket)
8	oz tomato sauce
1	cup water
1/2	tsp thyme
2	bay leaves
3/4	tsp salt
1/2	tsp pepper
1	tsp garlic powder
2	cups cooked rice

1. Heat the oil in a large saucepan and sauté the onion and bell pepper until slightly tender. Add the peas, tomato sauce, water, thyme, bay leaves, salt, pepper, and garlic powder and simmer 3 minutes.

2. Add the rice and stir well. Heat for 2 minutes or until the rice is hot.

EXCHANGES
1 1/2 Starch
1 Vegetable

Calories 135
    Calories from Fat 19
Total Fat . . . . 2 g
    Saturated Fat . . . . 0 g
Cholesterol . . . . 0 mg
Sodium . . . . 492 mg
Total Carbohydrate . . . . 25 g
    Dietary Fiber . . . . 4 g
    Sugars . . . . 4 g
Protein . . . . 4 g

Hoe Cake

Preparation time: 10 min   Serves 6   Serving size: 1 pancake

- 1 cup cornmeal
- 1 cup flour
- 2 tsp baking powder
- 1/2 tsp salt
- 2 Tbsp canola oil
- Cold water
- Nonstick cooking spray

1. Combine all dry ingredients and oil in a large bowl and add enough cold water to make a soft batter.

2. Spray a nonstick griddle with nonstick cooking spray and heat to medium heat. Pour the batter into the griddle and cook until done, turning once to brown both sides. Serve hot from the griddle.

EXCHANGES
2 Starch
1 Fat

Calories 204
   Calories from Fat 47
Total Fat . . . . 5 g
   Saturated Fat . . . . 0 g
Cholesterol . . . . 0 mg
Sodium . . . . 316 mg
Total Carbohydrate . . . . 35 g
   Dietary Fiber . . . . 2 g
   Sugars . . . . 0 g
Protein . . . . 4 g

Hoppin' John

Preparation time: 15 min   Serves 6   Serving size: 1 cup

1   lb dried black-eyed peas
2   qt water
1   medium onion, chopped
1   lb smoked turkey breast, chopped
    Red pepper flakes to taste (optional)
1   cup cooked rice

1. Soak the black-eyed peas overnight in cold water or boil for 2 minutes and then soak for 1 hour. Drain.

2. Place the peas in a large stockpot and add the water, onion, smoked turkey, and red pepper flakes. Simmer for 2 hours or until the peas are soft.

3. Stir in the rice or serve it on the side. (To reduce the sodium content of this recipe, use ground turkey breast instead of smoked turkey.)

EXCHANGES
3 1/2 Starch
3 Very Lean Meat

Calories 365
  Calories from Fat 17
Total Fat . . . . 2 g
  Saturated Fat . . . . 0 g
Cholesterol . . . . 35 mg
Sodium . . . . 920 mg
Total Carbohydrate . . . . 55 g
  Dietary Fiber . . . . 8 g
  Sugars . . . . 7 g
Protein . . . . 34 g

John's Garlic Rice

Preparation time: 15 min   Serves 8   Serving size: 1/2 cup

2   Tbsp reduced-fat margarine

2   Tbsp minced garlic

2   cups long-grain rice

4   cups reduced-sodium, reduced-fat chicken broth

Salt to taste (optional)

Pepper to taste (optional)

1. Heat the margarine in a large skillet and sauté the garlic and rice, stirring constantly, until lightly brown.

2. Add the chicken broth, salt, and pepper and stir. Bring to a boil; then reduce heat to simmer, cover, and cook for 20 minutes.

EXCHANGES

2 1/2 Starch

Calories 192
   Calories from Fat 15
Total Fat . . . . 2 g
   Saturated Fat . . . . 0 g
Cholesterol . . . . 0 mg
Sodium . . . . 301 mg
Total Carbohydrate . . . . 38 g
   Dietary Fiber . . . . 1 g
   Sugars . . . . 1 g
Protein . . . . 4 g

Red Rice

Preparation time: 15 min   Serves 6   Serving size: 1/2 cup

2	cups water
1	chicken-flavored bouillon cube
1	medium onion, chopped
1	cup uncooked rice
2	cloves garlic, minced
1/2	8-oz can tomato sauce
1	green bell pepper, seeded and chopped

1. Boil the water in a large saucepan. Add the bouillon cube and stir.

2. Add the remaining ingredients, stir well, and return to a boil. Reduce the heat to simmer and cook, covered, for 20 minutes.

EXCHANGES

2 Starch

Calories 137
  Calories from Fat 3
Total Fat . . . . 0 g
  Saturated Fat . . . . 0 g
Cholesterol . . . . 0 mg
Sodium . . . . 222 mg
Total Carbohydrate . . . . 30 g
  Dietary Fiber . . . . 1 g
  Sugars . . . . 4 g
Protein . . . . 3 g

Spanish Rice

2 Tbsp reduced-fat margarine

1 cup uncooked rice

1 medium onion, finely chopped

1/4 cup chopped celery

1 clove garlic, crushed

1 green bell pepper, seeded and chopped

2 cups water

1 14-oz can crushed tomatoes, undrained

1 tsp salt

1/4 tsp pepper

1. Heat the margarine in a large saucepan and sauté the rice, onion, celery, garlic, and bell pepper until the rice is lightly brown.

2. Add the water, tomatoes, salt, and pepper and bring to a boil. Reduce the heat to simmer and cook, covered, for 20 minutes.

EXCHANGES
1 1/2 Starch

Calories	130
Calories from Fat	15
Total Fat	2 g
Saturated Fat	0 g
Cholesterol	0 mg
Sodium	455 mg
Total Carbohydrate	26 g
Dietary Fiber	2 g
Sugars	4 g
Protein	3 g

Spoon Bread

1	cup boiling water
1	cup yellow cornmeal
1/2	tsp salt
2	tsp reduced-fat margarine
1	tsp baking powder
2	eggs, separated
1 1/2	cups nonfat milk

1. In a large heatproof bowl, pour the boiling water over the cornmeal and stir well. Stir the salt and margarine into the cornmeal and allow to cool.

2. Heat the oven to 375°F. Add the baking powder, egg yolks, and milk to the bowl and stir. Beat the egg whites until stiff peaks are formed and fold into the batter.

3. Pour the batter into a nonstick loaf pan and bake for 45 minutes.

EXCHANGES
1 1/2 Starch

Calories 137
   Calories from Fat 25
Total Fat . . . . 3 g
   Saturated Fat . . . . 1 g
Cholesterol . . . . 72 mg
Sodium . . . . 318 mg
Total Carbohydrate . . . . 21 g
   Dietary Fiber . . . . 2 g
   Sugars . . . . 3 g
Protein . . . . 6 g

Sweet Potato Bread

2	large sweet potatoes, peeled
2	Tbsp reduced-fat margarine
3	Tbsp sugar
1	tsp nutmeg
1 1/2	tsp allspice
1/4	tsp salt
5	Tbsp flour
1	cup egg substitute

1. Boil the sweet potatoes until soft and mash thoroughly. Stir in the margarine.

2. Heat the oven to 425°F. Add all ingredients and mix thoroughly.

3. Pour the batter into a nonstick loaf pan and bake for 30 minutes or until a knife inserted in the center comes out clean.

EXCHANGES
2 1/2 Starch

Calories	209
Calories from Fat	18
Total Fat	2 g
Saturated Fat	0 g
Cholesterol	0 mg
Sodium	212 mg
Total Carbohydrate	41 g
Dietary Fiber	4 g
Sugars	20 g
Protein	7 g

Soups and Salads

Black Bean Soup

1   lb dried black beans or 2 16-oz cans black beans, rinsed and drained

1   Tbsp canola oil

1   medium onion, chopped

4   cloves garlic, minced

1   carrot, shredded

1   green bell pepper, seeded and chopped

8   cups water

4   oz smoked turkey breast, diced

2   tsp oregano

1/2   tsp cumin

1/2   tsp pepper

1   tsp salt

2   Tbsp lemon juice

1. If using dried beans, soak them in water overnight. The next day, drain the beans.

2. In a large soup pot, heat the oil over medium heat. Add half the onion and all the garlic, carrot, and green pepper. Sauté until the vegetables are soft. Stir in the beans and water. Add the turkey, oregano, cumin, and pepper.

3. Cover and simmer for 30 minutes or until the beans are tender, stirring occasionally. Add the salt and lemon juice. Top with chopped onion to serve.

EXCHANGES
3 Starch
1 Very Lean Meat

Calories 225
   Calories from Fat 26
Total Fat . . . . 3 g
   Saturated Fat . . . . 0 g
Cholesterol . . . . 7 mg
Sodium . . . . 473 mg
Total Carbohydrate . . . . 42 g
   Dietary Fiber . . . . 10 g
   Sugars . . . . 5 g
Protein . . . . 17 g

Cabbage and Chicken Soup

Preparation time: 20 min   Serves 8   Serving size: 1 cup

4	cups water
3	cups reduced-sodium, reduced-fat chicken broth
2	cups chopped fresh tomatoes
1/2	stalk celery, chopped
4	stalks green onion, chopped
1	medium potato, peeled and diced
1	bay leaf
1	tsp salt
1/2	tsp thyme
1/4	tsp caraway seeds
3	cups shredded cabbage
1	cup cooked chopped chicken
1	Tbsp lemon juice
2	tsp sugar

1. In a large soup pot, combine the water, broth, tomatoes, celery, green onion, potato, bay leaf, salt, thyme, and caraway seeds.

2. Simmer for 30 minutes to 1 hour. Add the cabbage, chicken, lemon juice, and sugar. Remove the bay leaf and serve.

EXCHANGES
2 Vegetable
1 Very Lean Meat

Calories 81
  Calories from Fat 15
Total Fat . . . . 2 g
  Saturated Fat . . . . 1 g
Cholesterol . . . . 16 mg
Sodium . . . . 526 mg
Total Carbohydrate . . . . . 9 g
  Dietary Fiber . . . . 2 g
  Sugars . . . . 4 g
Protein . . . . 7 g

Barbecue Pulled Pork
Soul Slaw

Apple and Blueberry Tart

orn Soup, Cajun Style
Corn Muffins

Orange Sweet Potatoes

Chicken Gumbo Soup

Preparation time: 30 min   Serves 6   Serving size: 1 cup

1	lb boneless, skinless chicken breast, diced
3	cups reduced-sodium, reduced-fat chicken broth, divided
3	cups water
1	cup chopped onion
1	clove garlic, minced
1	tsp salt
1/2	tsp pepper
1	bay leaf
1/8	tsp sage
1/4	tsp red pepper flakes
1/4	tsp thyme
1	cup chopped fresh tomatoes
1	cup corn kernels, frozen or fresh
1	cup frozen okra
2	Tbsp canola oil
1/4	cup flour
2	cups cooked brown rice

1. Place the chicken in a large soup pot with 1 cup of broth. Bring to a boil.

2. Add the additional broth, water, onion, garlic, salt (omit this if you need to reduce total sodium), pepper, bay leaf, sage, red pepper flakes, and thyme and simmer for 20 minutes.

3. Add the tomatoes, corn, and okra and simmer for 15 minutes.

4. In a separate pan, heat the oil and flour and stir until the flour and oil are golden brown and bubbly, stirring constantly. Add 1 cup of the soup broth to the mixture and whisk until smooth.

5. Add the mixture back to the soup pot and whisk until dissolved. Simmer 30 minutes. Stir in the rice the last 10 minutes of cooking.

EXCHANGES
2 Starch
2 Lean Meat

Calories 279
  Calories from Fat 61
Total Fat . . . . 7 g
  Saturated Fat . . . . 0 g
Cholesterol . . . . 43 mg
Sodium . . . . 720 mg
Total Carbohydrate . . . . 31 g
  Dietary Fiber . . . . 4 g
  Sugars . . . . 5 g
Protein . . . . 23 g

Chicken Noodle Soup

Preparation time: 20 min	Serves 8	Serving size: 1 cup

8	cups reduced-sodium, reduced-fat chicken broth
1 1/2	cups cooked diced chicken
3	carrots, sliced
2	medium onions, diced
2	Tbsp lite soy sauce
1	Tbsp dry sherry
1/2	tsp ginger
1	Tbsp parsley
4	oz uncooked whole-wheat noodles
4	stalks green onion, chopped

1. Place the chicken broth in a large pot and bring to a boil.

2. Add the chicken, carrots, onion, soy sauce (omit this if you need to reduce total sodium), sherry, ginger, and parsley. Reduce the heat and simmer for 10 minutes.

3. Add the noodles and simmer for 10 minutes more. Top with green onion to serve.

EXCHANGES
1 Starch
2 Very Lean Meat

Calories 157
    Calories from Fat 24
Total Fat . . . . 3 g
    Saturated Fat . . . . 1 g
Cholesterol . . . . 37 mg
Sodium . . . . 751 mg
Total Carbohydrate . . . . 18 g
    Dietary Fiber . . . . 2 g
    Sugars . . . . 5 g
Protein . . . . 13 g

Corn Soup, Cajun Style

Preparation time: 30 min　　　　Serves 12　　　　Serving size: 1 cup

1	Tbsp canola oil
1 1/2	cups chopped onion
5	stalks green onion, sliced
1	cup chopped green bell pepper
2	cloves garlic, chopped
1/2	cup flour
5	cups water
4	chicken thighs, skinned, deboned, and chopped
1	14-oz can no-added-salt tomatoes, chopped (reserve juice)
2	cups chopped fresh tomatoes
6	oz tomato paste
1/8	tsp salt
1/8	tsp pepper
12	oz reduced-fat turkey sausage
32	oz frozen whole-kernel corn
4	oz lean boneless ham

1. Heat the oil in a large soup pot and sauté the onion, green onion, bell pepper, and garlic until tender. Add the flour and cook, stirring constantly, until bubbly.

2. Add the water, chicken, tomatoes and juice, tomato paste, salt, and pepper.

3. Brown the sausage in a separate skillet and drain. Add the sausage to the soup pot, along with the corn and ham. Bring to a boil, stirring frequently.

4. Reduce the heat and simmer, uncovered, for 1 hour, stirring occasionally.

EXCHANGES

1 1/2 Starch
2 Vegetable
1 Medium-Fat Meat

Calories	237
Calories from Fat	62
Total Fat	7 g
Saturated Fat	2 g
Cholesterol	38 mg
Sodium	487 mg
Total Carbohydrate	32 g
Dietary Fiber	4 g
Sugars	7 g
Protein	16 g

Cream of Broccoli Soup

Preparation time: 15 min　　　　Serves 6　　　　Serving size: 1 cup

1 1/2	cups water
3	cups finely chopped fresh broccoli
2	tsp canola oil
1	cup chopped onion
1	Tbsp chopped garlic
1	Tbsp flour
3	cups nonfat milk
1/2	tsp celery seeds
1	tsp salt
1/2	tsp pepper
1/8	tsp cayenne pepper
3/4	cup Parmesan cheese

1. Combine the water and the broccoli and boil over medium heat for 10 minutes. Remove from the heat and set aside.

2. In a large skillet, heat the oil and sauté the onion and garlic until translucent, about 5 minutes.

3. Add the flour to the skillet, stirring constantly to mix. Add the liquid from the broccoli and cook until thickened, about 10 minutes.

4. Add the milk, broccoli, and spices and stir well (omit the salt if you need to reduce total sodium). Cook until hot, but do not allow the milk to boil. Top each serving with 1 Tbsp Parmesan cheese.

EXCHANGES
1 Fat-Free Milk
1 Vegetable
1 Fat

Calories 146
　Calories from Fat 46
Total Fat . . . . 5 g
　Saturated Fat . . . . 2 g
Cholesterol . . . . 10 mg
Sodium . . . . 658 mg
Total Carbohydrate . . . . 15 g
　Dietary Fiber . . . . 3 g
　Sugars . . . . 9 g
Protein . . . . 11 g

Seafood Chowder

Preparation time: 35 min   Serves 6   Serving size: 1 cup

1	Tbsp	reduced-fat margarine
1 1/2	cups	chopped onion
1	Tbsp	chopped garlic
2	Tbsp	flour
2	cups	clam juice
2	cups	water
1/2	cup	chopped fresh parsley
2 1/2	cups	chopped potatoes
1	Tbsp	thyme
1/2	tsp	salt
1/2	tsp	pepper
1 1/2	lb	boneless, chopped flounder
2	cups	low-fat (1%) milk

1. In a large soup pot, melt the margarine and sauté the onion and garlic until translucent, about 5 minutes. Stir in the flour and cook for 2 minutes, stirring constantly. Add the clam juice and water.

2. Bring to a boil, stirring constantly. Add all ingredients except the fish and the milk. Simmer until the vegetables are tender, about 10 minutes.

3. Add the fish and the milk and simmer just until the fish turns opaque. Be careful not to boil the milk. Serve hot.

EXCHANGES
1 1/2 Starch
3 Very Lean Meat

Calories 231
  Calories from Fat 34
Total Fat . . . . 4 g
  Saturated Fat . . . . 0 g
Cholesterol . . . . 40 mg
Sodium . . . . 469 mg
Total Carbohydrate . . . . 21 g
  Dietary Fiber . . . . 2 g
  Sugars . . . . 6 g
Protein . . . . 28 g

Soulful Chili

Preparation time: 20 min   Serves 8   Serving size: 1 cup

2	tsp canola oil
2	medium onions, chopped
2	cloves garlic, minced
1	green bell pepper, seeded and chopped
1 1/2	lb 96% extra-lean ground beef
2 1/2	cups cooked kidney beans or 2 16-oz cans kidney beans, rinsed and drained
6	oz tomato paste
1	tsp reduced-sodium beef bouillon powder or one cube
1	Tbsp Worcestershire sauce
1	tsp dry mustard
	Red pepper flakes, to taste
3	Tbsp chili powder
	Salt to taste (optional)
	Pepper to taste (optional)
2	cups water

1. Heat the oil in a large soup pot and sauté the onion, garlic, and bell pepper for 5 minutes. Stir in the beef and cook until done.

2. Add the remaining ingredients, cover, and simmer for 20 minutes.

EXCHANGES

1 Starch
2 Vegetable
2 Lean Meat

Calories 243
  Calories from Fat 59
Total Fat . . . . 7 g
  Saturated Fat . . . . 2.1 g
Cholesterol . . . . 51 mg
Sodium . . . . 183 mg
Total Carbohydrate . . . . 24 g
  Dietary Fiber . . . . 6 g
  Sugars . . . . 5 g
Protein . . . . 23 g

Vegetable Soup with Noodles

Preparation time: 20 min   Serves 10   Serving size: 1 cup

1	Tbsp olive oil
2	cups chopped onion
1	green bell pepper, seeded and chopped
10	cups reduced-sodium, reduced-fat chicken broth
1	lb fresh carrots, sliced
1	cup chopped potatoes
1	cup fresh green beans, chopped
1	cup chopped fresh tomatoes
8	oz uncooked wide egg noodles
1/2	tsp pepper

1. Heat the oil in a large soup pot and sauté the onion and bell pepper until tender.

2. Add the vegetables and simmer for 20 minutes.

3. Add the noodles and pepper and simmer for 10 minutes or until the pasta is cooked.

EXCHANGES
1 1/2 Starch
1 Vegetable

Calories 174
  Calories from Fat 23
Total Fat . . . . 3 g
  Saturated Fat . . . . 1 g
Cholesterol . . . . 22 mg
Sodium . . . . 588 mg
Total Carbohydrate . . . . 30 g
  Dietary Fiber . . . . 4 g
  Sugars . . . . 6 g
Protein . . . . 7 g

Vegetarian Bean Stew

1	Tbsp canola oil
1	medium onion, chopped
2	cloves garlic, minced
2	cups sliced zucchini
1	cup chopped green bell pepper
1	tsp oregano
1/4	tsp salt
1/8	tsp pepper
2	cups chopped fresh tomatoes
1	16-oz can kidney beans, rinsed and drained
2	cups cooked brown rice
1/2	cup reduced-fat cheddar cheese

1. Heat the oil in a large soup pot and sauté the onion and garlic until tender. Add the zucchini, green pepper, oregano, salt, and pepper. Cook for 5 minutes.

2. Add the tomatoes and beans, cover, and heat thoroughly, about 15 minutes. Spoon the mixture over hot rice and sprinkle with cheese to serve.

EXCHANGES
1 1/2 Starch
2 Vegetable
1 Fat

Calories 219
   Calories from Fat 49
Total Fat . . . . 5 g
   Saturated Fat . . . . 1 g
Cholesterol . . . . 7 mg
Sodium . . . . 259 mg
Total Carbohydrate . . . . 34 g
   Dietary Fiber . . . . 6 g
   Sugars . . . . 7 g
Protein . . . . 10 g

Apple Slaw

1/4	cup reduced-fat sour cream
2	Tbsp sugar
1/2	tsp salt
1/2	tsp pepper
1	tsp ground mustard
2	lb unpeeled apples, julienned
2	Tbsp lemon juice
1	large head cabbage, julienned

1. In a large bowl, combine the sour cream, sugar, salt, pepper, and ground mustard. Mix well, cover, and chill for 1 hour.

2. Toss the apples with the lemon juice. Combine the apples and cabbage and mix well. Just before serving, add the dressing and toss.

EXCHANGES
1 1/2 Fruit
1 Vegetable

Calories 114
   Calories from Fat 12
Total Fat . . . . 1 g
   Saturated Fat . . . . 0 g
Cholesterol . . . . 3 mg
Sodium . . . . 173 mg
Total Carbohydrate . . . . 26 g
   Dietary Fiber . . . . 6 g
   Sugars . . . . 21 g
Protein . . . . 2 g

Cantaloupe Salad

Preparation time: 15 min   Serves 6   Serving size: 1 slice

1 cup reduced-fat whipped topping

3 Tbsp frozen orange juice concentrate, thawed and undiluted

1 medium cantaloupe

Lettuce leaves

1 cup seedless green grapes, halved

1. Combine the whipped topping and orange juice, mixing well.

2. Cut the cantaloupe into six sections, removing the seeds and peel. Place the cantaloupe on lettuce leaves; spoon grapes over and around each section.

3. Drizzle with the whipped topping mixture and serve.

EXCHANGES
1 Fruit
1/2 Fat

Calories 92
　Calories from Fat 16
Total Fat . . . . 2 g
　Saturated Fat . . . . 1 g
Cholesterol . . . . 0 mg
Sodium . . . . 12 mg
Total Carbohydrate . . . . 18 g
　Dietary Fiber . . . . 1 g
　Sugars . . . . 15 g
Protein . . . . 1 g

Chicken Salad

4	boneless, skinless chicken breast halves, cooked and cubed
1/3	cup reduced-fat mayonnaise
2	Tbsp cider vinegar
3/4	cup chopped celery
6	stalks green onion, chopped
1/2	cup chopped pecans
1/8	tsp garlic powder
1/4	tsp salt
1/8	tsp pepper
	Lettuce leaves

1. Combine all ingredients except the lettuce in a medium bowl and mix well.

2. Refrigerate until serving time. Serve on a bed of lettuce.

EXCHANGES
1/2 Starch
2 Very Lean Meat
2 Fat

Calories 213
  Calories from Fat 113
Total Fat . . . . 13 g
  Saturated Fat . . . . 1 g
Cholesterol . . . . 53 mg
Sodium . . . . 236 mg
Total Carbohydrate . . . . . 6 g
  Dietary Fiber . . . . 2 g
  Sugars . . . . 2 g
Protein . . . . 19 g

CJ's California Taco Salad

Preparation time: 20 min | Serves 12 | Serving size: 1 salad

1 1/2	lb 96% extra-lean ground beef or ground turkey breast
1	pkg taco seasoning mix
6	oz mild salsa
1/2	cup water
12	oz baked tortilla chips
1	medium head lettuce, shredded
3	large tomatoes, seeded and chopped
6	oz fat-free sour cream
6	oz fat-free shredded cheddar cheese

1. Brown the beef in a nonstick skillet until it crumbles. Drain the fat from the beef. Add the taco seasoning, salsa, and water. Reduce the heat and simmer for 5 minutes or until heated thoroughly.

2. Layer the salad on 12 plates in this order: chips, meat, lettuce, tomato, sour cream, and cheese. Add taco sauce, if desired.

EXCHANGES
1 1/2 Starch
1 Vegetable
2 Lean Meat

Calories 250
   Calories from Fat 43
Total Fat . . . . 5 g
   Saturated Fat . . . . 1.6 g
Cholesterol . . . . 37 mg
Sodium . . . . 542 mg
Total Carbohydrate . . . . 31 g
   Dietary Fiber . . . . 3 g
   Sugars . . . . 4 g
Protein . . . . 20 g

Creamy Salad Dressing

Preparation time: 5 min   Serves 8   Serving size: 1 Tbsp

1/4	cup fat-free plain yogurt
1/4	cup reduced-fat mayonnaise
1	Tbsp chopped garlic
2	tsp spicy brown mustard
2	Tbsp honey

Combine all ingredients, mixing well. Chill before serving.

EXCHANGES
1/2 Carbohydrate

Calories 46
Calories from Fat 21
Total Fat . . . . 2 g
Saturated Fat . . . . 1 g
Cholesterol . . . . 3 mg
Sodium . . . . 67 mg
Total Carbohydrate . . . . . 6 g
Dietary Fiber . . . . 0 g
Sugars . . . . 5 g
Protein . . . . 1 g

Fruit Salad

Preparation time: 20 min   Serves 12   Serving size: 1/2 cup

1 1/2	cups cubed cantaloupe
1 1/2	cups cubed honeydew melon
2	medium peaches, peeled and sliced
1	cup cubed fresh pineapple
1	cup grapes, halved
1	medium orange, peeled, seeded, and sliced
1	cup unsweetened Mandarin oranges
1	medium banana, sliced
16	oz fat-free sour cream
1/4	cup brown sugar
	Juice of 1 orange
	Juice of 1/2 lemon
3	Tbsp pineapple juice
1	tsp cinnamon

1. Combine the fruit except the banana in a large bowl and refrigerate.

2. Combine the remaining ingredients in a small bowl and mix well. Refrigerate.

3. To serve, add the bananas to the fruit. Toss with the dressing. Spoon into individual dishes.

EXCHANGES
1 1/2 Fruit

Calories 103
  Calories from Fat 3
Total Fat . . . . 0 g
  Saturated Fat . . . . 0 g
Cholesterol . . . . 0 mg
Sodium . . . . 48 mg
Total Carbohydrate . . . . 24 g
  Dietary Fiber . . . . 2 g
  Sugars . . . . 20 g
Protein . . . . 2 g

Green Pea Salad

Preparation time: 10 min   Serves 14   Serving size: 1/2 cup

1/2	cup reduced-fat mayonnaise
1	tsp Dijon mustard
1	tsp vinegar
1/8	tsp salt
1/8	tsp pepper
2	16-oz pkgs frozen green peas, thawed and drained
1	medium onion, finely chopped
2	eggs, boiled and chopped
1	tsp parsley

1. Combine the mayonnaise, mustard, vinegar, salt, and pepper in a small bowl and mix well.

2. Combine the peas, onion, and egg in a large bowl. Toss with the dressing and refrigerate. Sprinkle with parsley before serving.

EXCHANGES
1 Starch
1/2 Fat

Calories 88
   Calories from Fat 34
Total Fat . . . . 4 g
   Saturated Fat . . . . 0.7 g
Cholesterol . . . . 33 mg
Sodium . . . . 159 mg
Total Carbohydrate . . . . 10 g
   Dietary Fiber . . . . 3 g
   Sugars . . . . 4 g
Protein . . . . 4 g

Macaroni and Tuna Salad

    8   oz uncooked macaroni noodles
    1/2 cup reduced-fat mayonnaise
    1/2 cup fat-free sour cream
    2   tsp sugar
    2   Tbsp cider vinegar
    1   Tbsp prepared mustard
 1 1/2   cups chopped celery
    1/2 cup chopped onion
    1/3 cup chopped green bell pepper
    1   6-oz can water-packed tuna
    1   egg, boiled and chopped
    1/2 tsp salt
    1/2 tsp pepper

1. Cook the macaroni according to package directions (but without adding salt), drain thoroughly, and rinse in cold water.

2. Combine the mayonnaise, sour cream, sugar, vinegar, and mustard in a small bowl and mix well.

3. Combine all ingredients in a large bowl and toss well. Chill before serving.

EXCHANGES
2 Starch
1 Lean Meat

Calories 217
    Calories from Fat 53
Total Fat . . . . 6 g
    Saturated Fat . . . . 1 g
Cholesterol . . . . 39 mg
Sodium . . . . 392 mg
Total Carbohydrate . . . . 29 g
    Dietary Fiber . . . . 1 g
    Sugars . . . . 6 g
Protein . . . . 11 g

Mango Mango Salad with Chicken

Preparation time: 20 min   Serves 6   Serving size: 1 cup

1/3   cup reduced-fat mayonnaise
3   stalks green onion, chopped
2   cups cooked diced chicken breast
2   cups chopped ripe mango
1   green bell pepper, seeded and chopped
1   Tbsp apple cider vinegar
2   Tbsp lemon juice
1   tsp sugar
       Lettuce leaves

1. Combine the mayonnaise and green onion in a small bowl, cover, and chill. Combine the chicken, mango, and bell pepper in a large bowl.

2. Combine the vinegar, lemon juice, and sugar in a container with a tight lid. Shake well. Add the mayonnaise and green onion and stir well.

3. Pour the dressing over salad, toss well, and chill for 30 minutes. To serve, spoon onto a plate lined with lettuce leaves.

EXCHANGES
1/2 Fruit
1 Vegetable
2 Very Lean Meat
1 Fat

Calories 170
   Calories from Fat 57
Total Fat . . . . 6 g
   Saturated Fat . . . . 1.2 g
Cholesterol . . . . 44 mg
Sodium . . . . 150 mg
Total Carbohydrate . . . . 14 g
   Dietary Fiber . . . . 2 g
   Sugars . . . . 11 g
Protein . . . . 16 g

Potato Salad with Dill

Preparation time: 20 min   Serves 8   Serving size: 1/2 cup

2	cups diced boiled potatoes
1/2	cup chopped celery
1/4	cup chopped onion
1/4	cup chopped green bell pepper
1	cup reduced-calorie mayonnaise
2	Tbsp prepared mustard
2	Tbsp apple cider vinegar
2	Tbsp pickle relish
1/2	tsp salt
1/2	tsp pepper
1	tsp dill

1. Combine the potatoes, celery, onion, and bell pepper in a large bowl.

2. Combine the mayonnaise, mustard, vinegar, pickle relish, salt, pepper, and dill in a medium bowl and mix well.

3. Toss the vegetables with the dressing and refrigerate before serving, allowing the flavors to blend.

EXCHANGES
1 Starch

Calories 80
  Calories from Fat 28
Total Fat . . . . 3 g
  Saturated Fat . . . . 0.5 g
Cholesterol . . . . 3 mg
Sodium . . . . 326 mg
Total Carbohydrate . . . . 13 g
  Dietary Fiber . . . . 1 g
  Sugars . . . . 4 g
Protein . . . . 1 g

Seafood Salad

Preparation time: 20 min   Serves 12   Serving size: 1/2 cup

1/2	cup reduced-calorie mayonnaise
1/3	cup fat-free Italian salad dressing
2	Tbsp Parmesan cheese
1 1/2	cups cooked blue crabmeat, flaked, shell pieces removed
2	cups cooked pasta, any shape
1	cup blanched broccoli florets
1/2	cup chopped green or red bell pepper
1	cup chopped tomatoes
1/3	cup chopped onion

1. Combine the mayonnaise, salad dressing, and cheese in a small bowl and mix well.

2. Combine the remaining ingredients in a large bowl. Add the dressing and toss. Chill before serving.

EXCHANGES
1/2 Starch
1 Vegetable
1/2 Fat

Calories 94
  Calories from Fat 37
Total Fat . . . . 4 g
  Saturated Fat . . . . 0.8 g
Cholesterol . . . . 19 mg
Sodium . . . . 200 mg
Total Carbohydrate . . . . 10 g
  Dietary Fiber . . . . 1 g
  Sugars . . . . 2 g
Protein . . . . 5 g

Soul Slaw

Preparation time: 30 min   Serves 8   Serving size: 1 cup

1/2 cup reduced-fat mayonnaise
1/2 cup plain fat-free yogurt
1/4 cup apple cider vinegar
  2 tsp sugar
  2 Tbsp Dijon mustard
1/8 tsp salt
  1 tsp celery seeds
     Pepper to taste
  1 large head green cabbage, julienned
  2 medium raw carrots, grated

1. Combine the mayonnaise, yogurt, vinegar, sugar, mustard, salt, celery seeds, and pepper in a small bowl and mix well.

2. Combine the cabbage and carrots in a large bowl. Add the dressing, toss well, and refrigerate for at least 1 hour before serving.

EXCHANGES
3 Vegetable
1 Fat

Calories 108
  Calories from Fat 46
Total Fat . . . . 5 g
  Saturated Fat . . . . 1 g
Cholesterol . . . . 6 mg
Sodium . . . . 216 mg
Total Carbohydrate . . . . 14 g
  Dietary Fiber . . . . 4 g
  Sugars . . . . 9 g
Protein . . . . 3 g

Appetizers and Drinks

Celery with Shrimp

Preparation time: 15 min   Serves 16   Serving size: 1/2 stalk

1/2	lb cooked shrimp, chopped into chunky pieces
3	oz reduced-fat cream cheese, softened
2	Tbsp reduced-fat mayonnaise
1	Tbsp finely chopped onion
1	Tbsp finely chopped green bell pepper
1	Tbsp finely chopped green olive
	Dash Worcestershire sauce
	Dash hot pepper sauce
	Salt to taste (optional)
	Pepper to taste (optional)
8	celery stalks, cleaned, trimmed, and cut in half

Combine all ingredients and stuff the mixture into the celery stalks.

EXCHANGES
1 Very Lean Meat

Calories 37
   Calories from Fat 17
Total Fat . . . . 2 g
   Saturated Fat . . . . 1 g
Cholesterol . . . . 32 mg
Sodium . . . . 84 mg
Total Carbohydrate . . . . . 1 g
   Dietary Fiber . . . . 0 g
   Sugars . . . . 1 g
Protein . . . . 4 g

Chicken Puffs

Preparation time: 30 min   Serves 12   Serving size: 1 puff

1/4   cup boiling water
2   Tbsp reduced-fat margarine
1/4   cup flour
1/8   tsp salt
1/4   cup egg substitute
1/4   cup grated Swiss cheese
2   cups cooked chopped chicken breast
2   Tbsp chopped pimiento
2   Tbsp white wine
1/4   cup reduced-fat mayonnaise

1. Heat the oven to 400°F. Boil the water in a medium saucepan. Melt the margarine in the boiling water. Stir in the flour and salt.

2. Cook over medium heat, stirring vigorously, until the mixture forms a ball. Remove from the heat and let cool.

3. Add the egg substitute and beat for 1 minute. Drop the mixture by teaspoonfuls on a nonstick cookie sheet and bake for 20 minutes. Remove from the oven.

4. Combine the remaining ingredients and stuff the puff shells with the chicken salad mixture.

EXCHANGES
1 Very Lean Meat
1 Fat

Calories 84
   Calories from Fat 35
Total Fat . . . . 4 g
   Saturated Fat . . . . 1 g
Cholesterol . . . . 24 mg
Sodium . . . . 114 mg
Total Carbohydrate . . . . . 3 g
   Dietary Fiber . . . . 0 g
   Sugars . . . . 0 g
Protein . . . . 9 g

Cranberry-Lemon Relish

Preparation time: 10 min   Serves 8   Serving size: 1/4 cup

2	cups cranberries
1	large red apple, diced
1	small lemon, unpeeled, quartered, and seeded
1/2	cup sugar
1/4	tsp nutmeg
1/4	tsp cinnamon
1/4	tsp mace

1. Chop the cranberries, apple, and lemon in a blender or food processor just until chunky. Do not overblend.

2. Add the sugar and spices and stir until the sugar is dissolved. Chill before serving.

EXCHANGES
1 1/2 Carbohydrate

Calories 79
　Calories from Fat 2
Total Fat . . . . 0 g
　Saturated Fat . . . . 0 g
Cholesterol . . . . 0 mg
Sodium . . . . 1 mg
Total Carbohydrate . . . . 22 g
　Dietary Fiber . . . . 2 g
　Sugars . . . . 18 g
Protein . . . . 0 g

Golden Party Punch

3   oz orange-flavored, sugar-free gelatin

1   cup boiling water

6   oz canned frozen orange juice concentrate

2   cups pineapple juice

2   cups apple juice

12 oz diet ginger ale

1. Dissolve the gelatin in the boiling water. Mix in frozen concentrate and juices.

2. Stir in the ginger ale just before serving.

EXCHANGES
1 1/2 Fruit

Calories 102
  Calories from Fat 1
Total Fat . . . . 0 g
  Saturated Fat . . . . 0 g
Cholesterol . . . . 0 mg
Sodium . . . . 34 mg
Total Carbohydrate . . . . 24 g
  Dietary Fiber . . . . 0 g
  Sugars . . . . 23 g
Protein . . . . 1 g

Ham Roll

Preparation time: 15 min   Serves 8   Serving size: 1 ham roll

8   oz fat-free cream cheese, softened
2   Tbsp nonfat milk
1   Tbsp finely chopped parsley
8   thin slices boiled ham (about 1 lb)
1   16-oz jar pickled okra

1. Whip the cream cheese and milk in a blender or food processor until fluffy. Add the parsley.

2. Spread each ham slice with 1 oz of the cream cheese mixture. Place some pickled okra in the center of each slice and roll it up. Slice each ham roll in half to serve.

EXCHANGES
1 Vegetable
2 Very Lean Meat

Calories 92
    Calories from Fat 19
Total Fat . . . . 2 g
    Saturated Fat . . . . 1 g
Cholesterol . . . . 33 mg
Sodium . . . . 1161 mg
Total Carbohydrate . . . . . 5 g
    Dietary Fiber . . . . 1 g
    Sugars . . . . 2 g
Protein . . . . 14 g

Party Meatballs

Preparation time: 30 min   Serves 8   Serving size: 3 meatballs

1	lb extra-lean (95% fat-free) ground beef
1/2	cup bread crumbs
1/4	cup egg substitute
1	medium onion, finely chopped
1	Tbsp parsley
1	tsp Worcestershire sauce
1/4	cup nonfat milk
	Salt to taste (optional)
	Pepper to taste (optional)
2	tsp canola oil
1/4	cup reduced-fat, reduced-sodium chicken broth
1 1/4	cups reduced-calorie grape jelly or preserves
1/4	cup catsup

1. Mix the ground beef, bread crumbs, egg substitute, onion, parsley, Worcestershire sauce, milk, salt, and pepper together in a large bowl.

2. Roll into 24 1-inch balls. Heat the oil in a large skillet and brown the meatballs over medium heat. Stir in the chicken broth.

3. Meanwhile, melt the grape jelly or preserves and catsup together in a small saucepan over low heat until hot and pour over the meatballs. Cook for 30 minutes.

EXCHANGES
1 1/2 Carbohydrate
2 Very Lean Meat

Calories 191
 Calories from Fat 36
Total Fat . . . . 4 g
 Saturated Fat . . . . 0 g
Cholesterol . . . . 34 mg
Sodium . . . . 235 mg
Total Carbohydrate . . . . 23 g
 Dietary Fiber . . . . 1 g
 Sugars . . . . 9 g
Protein . . . . 14 g

Salmon Party Log

16	oz canned pink salmon, bones and skin removed, well drained
1	Tbsp lemon juice
1	tsp prepared horseradish
1/8	tsp liquid smoke seasoning (optional)
8	oz fat-free cream cheese, softened
2	Tbsp nonfat milk
2	tsp minced onion
1/4	tsp salt
1/2	cup finely chopped pecans
3	Tbsp chopped fresh parsley

1. Stir together the salmon, lemon juice, horseradish, liquid smoke, cream cheese, milk, onion, and salt. Cover and chill for 2 hours.

2. Shape the mixture into a 7-inch log. Stir the pecans and parsley together in a shallow dish.

3. Roll the log in the pecan mixture, wrap in plastic wrap, and chill. Serve with assorted crackers.

EXCHANGES
2 Medium-Fat Meat

Calories 154
   Calories from Fat 74
Total Fat . . . . 8 g
   Saturated Fat . . . . 0 g
Cholesterol . . . . 35 mg
Sodium . . . . 543 mg
Total Carbohydrate . . . . . 4 g
   Dietary Fiber . . . . 1 g
   Sugars . . . . 1 g
Protein . . . . 16 g

Salmon Spread

16	oz canned salmon, skin and bones removed, well drained
8	oz fat-free cream cheese, softened
1	Tbsp lemon juice
3	Tbsp grated onion
1	tsp liquid smoke seasoning
1/2	tsp mustard
1/2	tsp salt
2	Tbsp chopped fresh parsley

Flake the salmon and combine it with all the ingredients. Chill before serving with your favorite crackers.

EXCHANGES
1 Lean Meat

Calories 49
   Calories from Fat 15
Total Fat . . . . 2 g
   Saturated Fat . . . . 0.4 g
Cholesterol . . . . 12 mg
Sodium . . . . 275 mg
Total Carbohydrate . . . . . 1 g
   Dietary Fiber . . . . 0 g
   Sugars . . . . 1 g
Protein . . . . 7 g

Shrimp Dip

Preparation time: 15 min   Serves 16   Serving size: 1 Tbsp

2	Tbsp catsup
8	oz fat-free cream cheese, softened
1/2	cup minced onion
2	Tbsp reduced-fat mayonnaise
1	Tbsp lemon juice
1	tsp Worcestershire sauce
1	lb shelled, cooked shrimp, diced
3	sprigs fresh dill

1. Mix the catsup, cream cheese, onion, mayonnaise, lemon juice, and Worcestershire sauce together until well blended.

2. Add the shrimp and stir. Garnish with fresh dill and serve with low-sodium crackers.

EXCHANGES
1 Lean Meat

Calories 50
　Calories from Fat 8
Total Fat . . . . 1 g
　Saturated Fat . . . . 0 g
Cholesterol . . . . 54 mg
Sodium . . . . 173 mg
Total Carbohydrate . . . . . 2 g
　Dietary Fiber . . . . 0 g
　Sugars . . . . 1 g
Protein . . . . 8 g

Southern Spiced Tea

Preparation time: 10 min   Serves 8   Serving size: 1 cup

  6 cups boiling water
  3 Tbsp black tea
  1 cinnamon stick
  1 cup orange juice
  2 Tbsp lemon juice
1/2 cup sugar

1. Pour the boiling water over the tea and cinnamon. Steep for 10 minutes.

2. Strain the tea and add the remaining ingredients. The tea can be served hot or cold.

EXCHANGES
1 Carbohydrate

Calories 63
  Calories from Fat 0
Total Fat . . . . 0 g
  Saturated Fat . . . . 0 g
Cholesterol . . . . 0 mg
Sodium . . . . 1 mg
Total Carbohydrate . . . . 16 g
  Dietary Fiber . . . . 0 g
  Sugars . . . . 16 g
Protein . . . . 0 g

Spicy Shrimp Bites

Preparation time: 20 min   Serves 6   Serving size: 1/2 cup

1	lb medium-size raw shrimp, shelled and deveined
1	Tbsp rum
1/4	cup vinegar
2	Tbsp lite soy sauce
4	tsp sugar
2	tsp cornstarch
2	Tbsp canola oil
3	cloves garlic, minced
1/4	tsp red pepper flakes
1 1/2	Tbsp fresh minced ginger

1. Toss the shrimp with the rum. Combine the vinegar, soy sauce, sugar, and cornstarch in a small bowl and mix well.

2. Heat the canola oil in a wok or large skillet. When the oil gets hot, add the garlic, red pepper flakes, and ginger.

3. Add the shrimp and cook for 3 minutes until the sauce bubbles and thickens. Serve with toothpicks.

EXCHANGES
1/2 Carbohydrate
1 Medium-Fat Meat

Calories 114
   Calories from Fat 47
Total Fat . . . . 5 g
   Saturated Fat . . . . 0 g
Cholesterol . . . . 84 mg
Sodium . . . . 311 mg
Total Carbohydrate . . . . . 6 g
   Dietary Fiber . . . . 1 g
   Sugars . . . . 5 g
Protein . . . . 10 g

Strawberry Smoothie

Preparation time: 15 min   Serves 5   Serving size: 1 cup

3   cups cranberry juice cocktail

8   oz reduced-fat vanilla yogurt

1   pint fresh strawberries, cleaned, tops removed

1   banana, sliced

1. Combine half of all ingredients in a blender or food processor and blend or process until smooth.

2. Repeat with the remaining ingredients. Combine the mixtures together and pour into individual glasses to serve.

EXCHANGES
3 Fruit

Calories 174
  Calories from Fat 10
Total Fat . . . . 1 g
  Saturated Fat . . . . 0 g
Cholesterol . . . . 4 mg
Sodium . . . . 32 mg
Total Carbohydrate . . . . 40 g
  Dietary Fiber . . . . 2 g
  Sugars . . . . 35 g
Protein . . . . 3 g

Stuffed Strawberries

Preparation time: 20 min   Serves 20   Serving size: 1 strawberry

22   large fresh strawberries
3   oz fat-free cream cheese, softened
1   Tbsp nonfat milk
1   Tbsp finely chopped pecans
1 1/2   Tbsp powdered sugar
1   tsp almond liqueur

1. Dice two strawberries horizontally and set aside. Cut a thin slice from the stem end of each remaining strawberry, forming a base for the strawberry to stand on.

2. Cut each strawberry into four wedges starting at the pointed end. Be careful to cut to, but not through, the stem end.

3. Beat the cream cheese and milk at medium speed with an electric mixer until fluffy. Stir in the diced strawberries, pecans, powdered sugar, and almond liqueur.

4. Spoon about 1 tsp of the mixture into each strawberry. You can prepare the stuffing up to a day ahead, but do not stuff the strawberries more than 4 hours before serving.

EXCHANGES
Free

Calories 17
  Calories from Fat 3
Total Fat . . . . 0 g
  Saturated Fat . . . . 0 g
Cholesterol . . . . 1 mg
Sodium . . . . 24 mg
Total Carbohydrate . . . . . 3 g
  Dietary Fiber . . . . 1 g
  Sugars . . . . 2 g
Protein . . . . 1 g

Tangy Shrimp Dip

Preparation time: 15 min   Serves 16   Serving size: 1 Tbsp

        12   oz small curd, reduced-fat cottage cheese
        1/4   cup reduced-fat mayonnaise
        2   Tbsp chili sauce
        1   Tbsp lemon juice
        5   oz canned tiny shrimp, drained and well rinsed
        2   Tbsp diced onion
              Salt to taste (optional)
              Pepper to taste (optional)

1. Combine the cottage cheese, mayonnaise, chili sauce, and lemon juice. Beat until smooth.

2. Stir in the remaining ingredients. Chill thoroughly and serve with assorted crackers.

EXCHANGES
1 Lean Meat

Calories 45
   Calories from Fat 15
Total Fat . . . . 2 g
   Saturated Fat . . . . 1 g
Cholesterol . . . . 19 mg
Sodium . . . . 148 mg
Total Carbohydrate . . . . . 2 g
   Dietary Fiber . . . . 0 g
   Sugars . . . . 1 g
Protein . . . . 5 g

Tuna Ball

Preparation time: 15 min   Serves 8   Serving size: 1/8 recipe

2   6 1/2-oz cans water-packed tuna, well drained
4   oz fat-free cream cheese, softened
1   Tbsp pickle relish, drained
1   Tbsp finely chopped onion
1/2 cup chopped fresh parsley

1. Combine the tuna, cream cheese, relish, and onion in a bowl and mix until cream cheese is slightly chunky.

2. Form the mixture into a ball. Roll the ball in the parsley and chill before serving. Serve with pita bread wedges.

EXCHANGES
2 Very Lean Meat

Calories 65
   Calories from Fat 3
Total Fat . . . . 0 g
   Saturated Fat . . . . 0 g
Cholesterol . . . . 14 mg
Sodium . . . . 231 mg
Total Carbohydrate . . . . . 2 g
   Dietary Fiber . . . . 0 g
   Sugars . . . . 1 g
Protein . . . . 13 g

Desserts

Apple and Blueberry Tart

Preparation time: 20 min   Serves 8   Serving size: 1 slice

1 1/2	cups flour, lightly spooned into the measuring cup
1/4	tsp salt
6	Tbsp canola oil
3	Tbsp nonfat milk
2	green apples, peeled and thinly sliced (about 3 cups)
1	cup fresh blueberries
1	Tbsp lemon juice
1/3	cup brown sugar
1	Tbsp flour
3/4	tsp cinnamon

1. Mix the flour and salt together. Combine oil and milk; add to flour and stir lightly with a fork. Form into a ball and flatten slightly between two squares of waxed paper. Roll into an 11-inch circle. Refrigerate while preparing filling.

2. Heat the oven to 425°F. Place the fruit in a bowl and toss with the lemon juice. Add the brown sugar, 1 Tbsp flour, and cinnamon, and mix well.

3. Peel off the top sheet of waxed paper and place dough, paper side up, on a large pizza pan. Discard waxed paper, and arrange fruit on the center of the dough, leaving a 2-inch border. Fold the edge of the pastry up and over the fruit, overlapping to form the sides. Pinch together any pastry that breaks to prevent leaking. Bake for 20–30 minutes, until apples are tender. If tart browns too quickly, cover with foil. Cool 10 minutes and serve.

EXCHANGES

2 1/2 Carbohydrate
1 1/2 Fat

Calories 249
  Calories from Fat 95
Total Fat . . . . 11 g
  Saturated Fat . . . . 0.8 g
Cholesterol . . . . 0 mg
Sodium . . . . 81 mg
Total Carbohydrate . . . . 37 g
  Dietary Fiber . . . . 2 g
  Sugars . . . . 16 g
Protein . . . . 3 g

Apple Crisp

Preparation time: 20 min   Serves 6   Serving size: 1/2 cup

	Nonstick cooking spray
4	large baking apples, peeled and sliced
3/4	cup brown sugar
1/2	cup flour
3/4	cup oatmeal
3/4	tsp cinnamon
3/4	tsp nutmeg
1/3	cup reduced-fat margarine

1. Heat the oven to 350°F. Spray a baking pan with nonstick cooking spray and place the apples in the pan.

2. Mix the brown sugar, flour, oatmeal, cinnamon, and nutmeg together and place on top of the apple. Drop dots of margarine over the dry mixture. Bake for 25 minutes.

EXCHANGES
4 Carbohydrate
1 Fat

Calories	298
Calories from Fat	55
Total Fat	6 g
Saturated Fat	1 g
Cholesterol	0 mg
Sodium	91 mg
Total Carbohydrate	61 g
Dietary Fiber	4 g
Sugars	44 g
Protein	3 g

Aunt Dorothy's Tea Cakes

Preparation time: 20 min   Serves 12   Serving size: 1 tea cake

1/2   cup reduced-fat margarine
3/4   cup sugar
1/2   cup egg substitute
1/2   cup low-fat buttermilk
1/4   cup molasses
  2   cups flour
1/2   tsp baking soda
  1   tsp baking powder
1/2   tsp nutmeg

1. Heat the oven to 375°F. Cream the margarine and sugar together. Add 1/4 cup of egg substitute and mix well, then add another 1/4 cup and mix well.

2. Combine the buttermilk and molasses. In a separate bowl, combine the dry ingredients. Alternately add buttermilk and flour portions to the margarine mixture until all the portions are added.

3. Drop the batter by spoonfuls onto a nonstick baking sheet. Bake for 12–15 minutes.

EXCHANGES
2 1/2 Carbohydrate
1/2 Fat

Calories 187
  Calories from Fat 36
Total Fat . . . . 4 g
  Saturated Fat . . . . 1 g
Cholesterol . . . . 0 mg
Sodium . . . . 175 mg
Total Carbohydrate . . . . 34 g
  Dietary Fiber . . . . 1 g
  Sugars . . . . 18 g
Protein . . . . 4 g

Baked Apples

Preparation time: 20 min   Serves 6   Serving size: 1 apple

6   medium baking apples
1/4 cup boiling water
1/3 cup sugar
1   tsp cinnamon
2   Tbsp reduced-fat margarine

1. Heat the oven to 350°F. Wash and core the apples, but do not peel them. Place the apples in a nonstick baking dish.

2. Add the water to the apples. Mix the sugar and cinnamon together and spoon into the cavity of the apples. Add margarine to each cavity.

3. Cover and bake for 30 minutes or until the apples are tender. Serve hot.

EXCHANGES
2 Carbohydrate
1/2 Fat

Calories 152
　Calories from Fat 22
Total Fat . . . . 2 g
　Saturated Fat . . . . 0 g
Cholesterol . . . . 0 mg
Sodium . . . . 30 mg
Total Carbohydrate . . . . 35 g
　Dietary Fiber . . . . 4 g
　Sugars . . . . 31 g
Protein . . . . 0 g

Bananas Foster

Preparation time: 15 min   Serves 4   Serving size: 1 banana

2 Tbsp reduced-fat margarine

4 small bananas

2 Tbsp brown sugar

   Dash ground cinnamon

1 Tbsp banana liqueur

1/2 cup fat-free, sugar-free, rum-flavored ice cream

1. Melt the margarine in a small skillet. Cut the bananas in half and brown in the margarine.

2. Sprinkle the bananas with the brown sugar, cinnamon, and liqueur and set aflame. Serve blazing with ice cream.

EXCHANGES
2 Carbohydrate
1/2 Fat

Calories 145
  Calories from Fat 28
Total Fat . . . . 3 g
  Saturated Fat . . . . 1 g
Cholesterol . . . . 0 mg
Sodium . . . . 68 mg
Total Carbohydrate . . . . 30 g
  Dietary Fiber . . . . 2 g
  Sugars . . . . 21 g
Protein . . . . 2 g

Bread Pudding

Preparation time: 20 min   Serves 8   Serving size: 1/2 cup

1/2	cup raisins
6	cups whole-wheat bread, cubed
1	16-oz can peaches packed in their own juice, drained
1	cup sugar
2	tsp vanilla
2	tsp butter-flavored extract
1	cup egg substitute
2	13-oz cans fat-free (skim) evaporated milk plus water to make 4 cups
1	tsp cinnamon
1	tsp nutmeg
1	tsp lemon juice

1. Heat the oven to 350°F. Layer the raisins, bread, and peaches in a 3-quart nonstick baking dish (or spray the dish with nonstick cooking spray).

2. Beat the remaining ingredients together and pour the mixture over the bread and peaches. Place the dish in a hot water bath and bake for 45 minutes or until a toothpick inserted in the center comes out clean.

EXCHANGES
4 Carbohydrate

Calories 283
   Calories from Fat 10
Total Fat . . . . 1 g
   Saturated Fat . . . . 0 g
Cholesterol . . . . 3 mg
Sodium . . . . 274 mg
Total Carbohydrate . . . . 58 g
   Dietary Fiber . . . . 2 g
   Sugars . . . . 45 g
Protein . . . . 13 g

Candace's Fruit Delight

Preparation time: 20 min   Serves 6   Serving size: 3/4 cup

2	Tbsp honey
3	Tbsp lemon juice
1 1/4	tsp cinnamon
2 1/2	cups bite-sized watermelon pieces
1/2	cup orange sections
1	cup sliced strawberries
1/2	cup halved seedless grapes

1. Combine the honey, lemon juice, and cinnamon in a small bowl and mix well. Chill until cold.

2. Combine the fruit and toss with the dressing. Serve on a bed of lettuce.

EXCHANGES
1 Fruit

Calories	67
Calories from Fat	4
Total Fat	0 g
Saturated Fat	0 g
Cholesterol	0 mg
Sodium	4 mg
Total Carbohydrate	17 g
Dietary Fiber	1 g
Sugars	15 g
Protein	1 g

Cheesecake Tarts

Preparation time: 20 min   Serves 10   Serving size: 1 tart

    2   8-oz pkg fat-free cream cheese, softened
  1/2   cup sugar
    1   cup egg substitute
    1   tsp vanilla
    2   tsp lemon juice
   12   vanilla wafers

1. Heat the oven to 350°F. Whip the cream cheese for 2 minutes or until fluffy. Add the sugar, egg substitute, vanilla, and lemon juice. Mix well.

2. Place 10 aluminum cupcake holders in muffin tins. Place a vanilla wafer in the bottom of each holder and pour the batter over each vanilla wafer.

3. Bake for 20 minutes. Remove from the heat and cool. If desired, top each tart with 1 tsp of jam or jelly (not included in nutritional analysis).

EXCHANGES
1 1/2 Carbohydrate

Calories 116
  Calories from Fat 6
Total Fat . . . . 1 g
  Saturated Fat . . . . 0 g
Cholesterol . . . . 8 mg
Sodium . . . . 311 mg
Total Carbohydrate . . . . 17 g
  Dietary Fiber . . . . 0 g
  Sugars . . . . 13 g
Protein . . . . 10 g

Fruit Cup

1/2   cup honeydew balls

1/2   cup cantaloupe balls

1/2   cup halved fresh strawberries

3   Tbsp orange liqueur

Fresh mint leaves

1. Combine all the ingredients except the mint. Toss gently to coat. Cover and chill for 2 hours.

2. Spoon into individual compote dishes and garnish with mint leaves to serve.

EXCHANGES

2 Carbohydrate

Calories 128
  Calories from Fat 3
Total Fat . . . . 0 g
  Saturated Fat . . . . 0 g
Cholesterol . . . . 0 mg
Sodium . . . . 10 mg
Total Carbohydrate . . . . 22 g
  Dietary Fiber . . . . 1 g
  Sugars . . . . 21 g
Protein . . . . 1 g

Jeanette's Custard

Preparation time: 10 min   Serves 4   Serving size: 1/2 cup

2 eggs

3 Tbsp sugar

1 tsp vanilla

1 2/3 cups nonfat milk

1/2 tsp nutmeg

1. Heat the oven to 325°F. Combine the eggs, sugar, vanilla, and milk in a medium bowl. Beat well and pour into individual custard cups or a baking dish.

2. Sprinkle nutmeg over the mixture and bake for 35 minutes. The custard is done when a knife inserted in the center of the custard comes out clean.

EXCHANGES
1 Carbohydrate
1/2 Fat

Calories	109
Calories from Fat	24
Total Fat	3 g
Saturated Fat	1 g
Cholesterol	108 mg
Sodium	84 mg
Total Carbohydrate	15 g
Dietary Fiber	0 g
Sugars	14 g
Protein	7 g

Key Lime Pie

Preparation time: 20 min   Serves 8   Serving size: 1 slice

1 3/4	cups graham cracker crumbs
4	Tbsp 60% vegetable oil spread (such as Olivio)
3	eggs, separated
1	12-oz can fat-free (skim) evaporated milk
1	Tbsp cornstarch
1/3	cup sugar
1/3	cup fresh key lime juice
3	drops green food coloring
1/4	cup sugar

1. Preheat the oven to 350°F. Combine the graham cracker crumbs and vegetable oil spread in a medium bowl and cut to mix. Press into a 9-inch pie pan and bake for 7–10 minutes or until browned.

2. Combine egg yolks, milk, cornstarch, and 1/3 cup sugar in a saucepan. Cook over medium heat, bringing the mixture to a boil. Remove from the heat and add the lime juice and the food coloring. Pour the mixture into the crust.

3. Beat the egg whites with a mixer until peaks form. Add 1/4 cup sugar and beat until stiff.

4. Spoon the meringue over the filling and bake until the edges are lightly brown, about 15 minutes. Cool before serving.

EXCHANGES
2 1/2 Carbohydrate
1 Fat

Calories	242
Calories from Fat	70
Total Fat	8 g
Saturated Fat	1.4 g
Cholesterol	79 mg
Sodium	246 mg
Total Carbohydrate	35 g
Dietary Fiber	1 g
Sugars	22 g
Protein	7 g

Pineapple Upside-Down Cake

Preparation time: 20 min   Serves 8   Serving size: 1 piece

Nonstick cooking spray
8 pineapple rings packed in their own juice
2 Tbsp molasses
1/3 cup reduced-fat margarine
1/2 cup honey
2 egg whites
1 1/2 cups flour
1/2 tsp baking soda
3/4 cup pineapple juice (use the juice from the pineapple rings and add water, if necessary)

1. Heat the oven to 350°F. Spray a 9-inch baking pan with nonstick cooking spray. Arrange the pineapple rings on the bottom of the pan. Pour the molasses over the pineapple.

2. In a separate bowl, beat the margarine, honey, and egg whites. Add the remaining ingredients and stir until smooth. Pour the batter over the pineapple.

3. Bake for 30–35 minutes. Cool before serving.

EXCHANGES
3 Carbohydrate
1/2 Fat

Calories 237
   Calories from Fat 36
Total Fat . . . . 4 g
   Saturated Fat . . . . 1 g
Cholesterol . . . . 0 mg
Sodium . . . . 156 mg
Total Carbohydrate . . . . 48 g
   Dietary Fiber . . . . 1 g
   Sugars . . . . 29 g
Protein . . . . 4 g

Red Velvet Cake

Preparation time: 30 min Serves 24 Serving size: 1 square

1/2	cup shortening
1	cup sugar
1	cup egg substitute
2	Tbsp cocoa
1 1/2	Tbsp red food coloring
1	tsp vanilla
2 1/2	cups flour
1/2	tsp salt
1	tsp baking soda
1	cup nonfat buttermilk
1	Tbsp vinegar
1	cup reduced-fat whipped topping (optional)

1. Heat the oven to 350°F. Cream the shortening, sugar, and egg substitute together. In a small bowl, make a thick paste of the cocoa and food coloring and add it to the cream mixture. Stir in the vanilla.

2. Sift together the flour, salt, and baking soda. Alternately add portions of the flour mixture and the buttermilk to the creamed mixture, stirring well.

3. Mix in the vinegar and pour the batter into a 13 × 9-inch or oblong pan. Bake for 30 minutes. Allow to cool. Cut into 24 squares and top each square with whipped topping.

EXCHANGES
1 Carbohydrate
1 Fat

Calories 127
   Calories from Fat 41
Total Fat . . . . 5 g
   Saturated Fat . . . . 1.2 g
Cholesterol . . . . 0 mg
Sodium . . . . 131 mg
Total Carbohydrate . . . . 19 g
   Dietary Fiber . . . . 1 g
   Sugars . . . . 9 g
Protein . . . . 3 g

Rice Pudding

1 1/2	cups cooked rice
3/4	cup raisins
1/2	cup sugar
2	eggs
3/4	cup egg substitute
1	tsp vanilla
1	tsp cinnamon
	Dash nutmeg
2	cups nonfat milk, scalded
2	tsp melted reduced-fat margarine

1. Heat the oven to 350°F. Combine the rice, raisins, sugar, eggs, egg substitute, vanilla, cinnamon, and nutmeg in a large bowl.

2. Add the milk and margarine and mix well. Pour the batter into a 1 1/2-quart casserole.

3. Place the casserole in a hot water bath and bake for 1 hour or until the pudding is firm.

EXCHANGES
2 Carbohydrate

Calories 148
    Calories from Fat 14
Total Fat . . . . 2 g
    Saturated Fat . . . . 0 g
Cholesterol . . . . 43 mg
Sodium . . . . 78 mg
Total Carbohydrate . . . . 28 g
    Dietary Fiber . . . . 1 g
    Sugars . . . . 20 g
Protein . . . . 6 g

Skillet Peach Upside-Down Cake

Preparation time: 25 min   Serves 10   Serving size: 1 slice

1/3	cup reduced-fat margarine
1/2	cup brown sugar
1/2	cup sugar
1	16-oz can sliced peaches, packed in their own juice
4	maraschino cherries, sliced
1	cup egg substitute
2/3	cup nonfat milk
1 1/2	cups flour
3	tsp baking powder
1/8	tsp salt

1. Heat the oven to 350°F. Melt the margarine and sugars in a small saucepan until the sugars are dissolved. Remove from the heat.

2. Drain the peaches and place them in the center of a heavy ovenproof skillet or 9-inch cake pan, forming a circle. Sprinkle the cherries on top.

3. Add the egg substitute and milk to the sugar mixture. In a separate bowl, combine the flour, baking powder, and salt. Add the flour in increments to the sugar mixture and mix well.

4. Pour the batter over the peaches and bake for 40 minutes.

EXCHANGES
3 Carbohydrate

Calories	215
Calories from Fat	29
Total Fat	3 g
Saturated Fat	1 g
Cholesterol	0 mg
Sodium	189 mg
Total Carbohydrate	42 g
Dietary Fiber	1 g
Sugars	27 g
Protein	5 g

Sponge Cake

Preparation time: 20 min   Serves 12   Serving size: 1 slice

7	egg whites and yolks
1 1/4	cups sugar
1/3	cup nonfat milk, scalded, slightly cooled
1	tsp vanilla
1	Tbsp lemon juice
1	cup cake flour

1. Heat the oven to 350°F. Beat the egg whites until stiff. In a separate bowl, mix the egg yolks and sugar until the mixture is creamy and lemon colored.

2. Add the milk, vanilla, and lemon juice to the egg yolk mixture and beat well. Fold the flour by spoonfuls into the mixture. Fold in the egg whites.

3. Bake for 40 minutes or until the cake springs back to the touch.

EXCHANGES
2 Carbohydrate
1/2 Fat

Calories 168
   Calories from Fat 27
Total Fat . . . . 3 g
   Saturated Fat . . . . 1 g
Cholesterol . . . . 124 mg
Sodium . . . . 41 mg
Total Carbohydrate . . . . 31 g
   Dietary Fiber . . . . 0 g
   Sugars . . . . 22 g
Protein . . . . 5 g

Strawberry Cake

Preparation time: 15 min   Serves 6   Serving size: 1/2 cup

6	ladyfingers or 1 small sponge cake
1 1/4	cup sliced fresh strawberries
3	Tbsp sugar
1/2	tsp vanilla
1/3	cup reduced-fat whipped topping
1	Tbsp chopped walnuts

1. Line a medium glass dish with split ladyfingers or sliced sponge cake. In a small bowl, toss the strawberries with the sugar.

2. In a separate bowl, add the vanilla to the whipped topping. Sprinkle some berries over the cake, then add a layer of whipped topping. Sprinkle with nuts.

3. Repeat in layers until all ingredients are used, ending with a layer of whipped topping and nuts.

EXCHANGES
1 Carbohydrate
1/2 Fat

Calories 97
   Calories from Fat 20
Total Fat . . . . 2 g
   Saturated Fat . . . . 0 g
Cholesterol . . . . 47 mg
Sodium . . . . 20 mg
Total Carbohydrate . . . . 18 g
   Dietary Fiber . . . . 1 g
   Sugars . . . . 13 g
Protein . . . . 1 g

Strawberry Cream

2　0.3-oz pkgs sugar-free strawberry-flavored gelatin

2　cups boiling water

12　oz sugar-free lemon-lime soda

2　cups fat-free whipped topping

1. Dissolve the gelatin in the boiling water. Stir in the soda and chill until almost firm.

2. Whip the mixture until foamy and fold in whipped topping. Place the mixture into a large glass bowl or individual serving dishes and chill until firm.

EXCHANGES
1/2 Carbohydrate

Calories 26
　Calories from Fat 0
Total Fat . . . . 0 g
　Saturated Fat . . . . 0 g
Cholesterol . . . . 0 mg
Sodium . . . . 48 mg
Total Carbohydrate . . . . . 4 g
　Dietary Fiber . . . . 0 g
　Sugars . . . . 1 g
Protein . . . . 1 g

Sweet Potato Pie

Preparation time: 20 min   Serves 10   Serving size: 1 piece

3	large cooked sweet potatoes, peeled and mashed
3/4	cup sugar
1/2	cup egg substitute
2	tsp vanilla
1	tsp lemon-flavored extract
1	Tbsp butter-flavored extract
1	tsp cinnamon
1	tsp nutmeg
1/8	cup brandy
1	tsp lemon juice
1 1/2	cups fat-free (skim) evaporated milk
1	9-inch pie shell

1. Heat the oven to 350°F.

2. Mix all the ingredients together and beat until smooth. Pour into the pie shell and bake for 40 minutes.

EXCHANGES
3 1/2 Carbohydrate
1/2 Fat

Calories 270
   Calories from Fat 39
Total Fat . . . . 4 g
   Saturated Fat . . . . 1 g
Cholesterol . . . . 1 mg
Sodium . . . . 159 mg
Total Carbohydrate . . . . 52 g
   Dietary Fiber . . . . 3 g
   Sugars . . . . 31 g
Protein . . . . 7 g

Sweet Potato Pound Cake

Preparation time: 25 min   Serves 12   Serving size: 1 slice

- 1 cup reduced-fat margarine
- 1 cup sugar
- 1 cup brown sugar
- 2 1/2 cups cooked, mashed sweet potatoes
- 1 cup egg substitute
- 2 tsp vanilla
- 3 cups flour
- 1 tsp salt
- 1 tsp baking soda
- 2 tsp butter-flavored extract
- 1 tsp nutmeg
- 1 tsp cinnamon

1. Heat the oven to 350°F. Cream the margarine and sugars in a large bowl until fluffy. Add the sweet potatoes, egg substitute, and vanilla and beat for 2 minutes.

2. Add the remaining ingredients and mix well. Pour the batter into a nonstick loaf pan and bake for 1 hour or until a toothpick inserted in the center comes out clean.

EXCHANGES
4 1/2 Carbohydrate
1 Fat

Calories 370
  Calories from Fat 70
Total Fat . . . . 8 g
  Saturated Fat . . . . 1 g
Cholesterol . . . . 0 mg
Sodium . . . . 467 mg
Total Carbohydrate . . . . 70 g
  Dietary Fiber . . . . 2 g
  Sugars . . . . 40 g
Protein . . . . 6 g

Index

ALPHABETICAL LIST OF RECIPES

SUBJECT INDEX

Other Titles Available from Small Steps Press

What to Eat When You're Eating Out

By Hope S. Warshaw, MMSc, RD

This comprehensive book provides complete nutrition information for more than 5,000 menu items from more than 60 restaurants, along with strategies for choosing healthier foods when eating out.

Order #4723-01
$9.95 US

The Healthy Lunchbox: How to Plan, Prepare, and Pack Stress-Free Meals Kids Will Love

By Marie McClendon, MEd, and Cristy Shauck

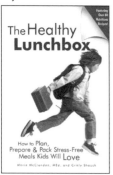

Do your kids groan when they look inside their lunchboxes? Do the nutritious meals you pack return home uneaten? Are you having trouble finding suitable and tasty recipes for your child with special eating needs? This unique guide is filled with helpful tips, tricks, and techniques for preparing quick and easy healthy meals.

Order #5013-01
$12.95 US

The Ultimate Calorie, Carb, and Fat Gram Counter

By Lea Ann Holzmeister, RD, CDE

If you want to lose weight or just keep track of how much fat or how many carbs you're eating, let this handy reference be your guide. Packed with information, this book features nutrient counts for more than 7,000 fresh, packaged, and restaurant foods.

Order #4724-01
$9.95 US

Disease Prevention Cookbook

By Clara Schneider, MS, RD, RN, LD, CDE

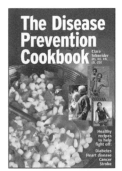

This innovative cookbook is filled with delicious recipes and tools designed to help you prevent some of the most prevalent diseases in our society, including diabetes, heart disease, stroke, and cancer.

Order #4651-01

$14.95 US

200 Healthy Recipes in 30 Minutes—Or Less!

By Robyn Webb, MS

Don't let the time crunch of today's modern lifestyle get in the way of eating healthy foods and enjoying tasty meals. With the help of Robyn Webb, you'll never run out of quick, healthy recipes that will satisfy even the most picky eater!

Order #4654-01

$16.95 US

To order these and other great **Small Steps Press** titles, call **1-800-232-6733** or visit **http://store.diabetes.org**. **Small Steps Press** titles are also available in bookstores nationwide.